Screwed-Up School Reform

Fixing America's Broken Promise

Richard G. Shear and Bruce S. Cooper

ROWMAN & LITTLEFIELD EDUCATION
A division of
ROWMAN & LITTLEFIELD PUBLISHERS, INC.
Lanham • New York • Toronto • Plymouth, UK

Published by Rowman & Littlefield Education
A division of Rowman & Littlefield Publishers, Inc.
A wholly owned subsidiary of The Rowman & Littlefield Publishing Group, Inc.
4501 Forbes Boulevard, Suite 200, Lanham, Maryland 20706
www.rowman.com

10 Thornbury Road, Plymouth PL6 7PP, United Kingdom

British Library Cataloguing in Publication Information Available

Library of Congress Cataloging-in-Publication Data

Library of Congress Cataloging-in-Publication Data Available
ISBN 978-1-61048-601-9 (pbk. : alk. paper)—978-1-61048-602-6 (electronic)

♾™ The paper used in this publication meets the minimum requirements of American
National Standard for Information Sciences Permanence of Paper for Printed Library
Materials, ANSI/NISO Z39.48-1992.

Printed in the United States of America

Contents

Preface

The unspoken promise of America is that each generation will have a better life than the previous one. The fulfillment of this promise has long been found behind the schoolhouse door. In America, a better education meant a better life. But for today's children, decades of failed school reform have left a generation wondering if the promise has been broken.

Attempts to reform and improve American schools are hardly new. In fact, starting with major efforts in the 1950s and 1960s following the *Brown* (1953) decision to desegregate schools, through the Lyndon Johnson presidency with passage of the Elementary and Secondary Education Act (ESEA), and into the twenty-first century, all levels of government have worked to raise standards, bolster schools, improve student performance, and bring U.S. education to its full potential.

So why aren't schools better, despite these policies, programs, and resources? What's missing from the equation? We argue in this book that it's the children, who are somehow overlooked in all the programs and effort. For we see that generations of school reforms have actively worked to cure the symptoms of "broken schools" but not the systemic problems that permeate the system.

As psychiatrist William Glasser (1986) wrote, "American students are committing 'educational suicide' as a result of having their thoughts, opinions, and needs disregarded by the public schools" (p. 11). Back in 1986, he explained in *Control Theory in the Classroom*, "We are far too concerned with discipline, with how to 'make' students follow rules, and not enough concerned with providing the satisfying education that would make our over-concern with discipline unnecessary" (p. 426).

The problem with a generation of school reform is that it has been actively working to cure the symptoms of broken schools and not the disease that has permeated the system. Virtually an entire society has failed to perceive the main problem with American education is that children are rejecting practices, treatment, and conditions within their schools. All other issues in schooling pale in comparison with the fact that too many kids "hate the product."

The reality is we have to understand why past reform efforts have failed to "fix the problem." The problems of our public schools have been considered for over a century. So the question arises, why are we so concerned today? What is the new risk to our society if we continue to conduct business in the same broken way?

Perhaps to clarify the risk we are facing, we can best understand the consequences by making a comparison to a past historical situation. Fifty years ago, the Soviet Union was involved in a space race with the United States. When President Kennedy declared that by the end of the decade, the United States would land a man on the moon, the space race was on. The problem for the United States was that the Soviet Union already had a half-decade lead on America in the race to the moon.

Today, everyone knows the Soviets lost in their pursuit of the moon and in fact never got there at all; all this failure occurred despite their major advantage in space at the beginning of the decade. The Soviet leaders simply could not make appropriate adjustments to their space program due to their inability to recognize the real problem. Just like American educational reformers in today's world, the Soviets were seeking solutions based only on existing practices.

Few realized that the essential problem the Soviets and the Americans faced would require thinking outside of the box. Thinking out of the box was something that American engineers were much more comfortable with than Soviet engineers. Soviet engineers of the 1960s thought like American school reformers of today.

Just as today's American educators, politicians, and pundits have failed in their efforts to fix the public schools, the Russians lost the space race. Both failed because they could not change their traditional view of what a solution should look like. The Russians could not change what they thought a moon landing would look like. The American school reformers have been unable to change what the public schools should look like.

In the case of the space race, the Russians refused to reconsider the conventional paradigm of one rocket ship leaving earth, landing on the moon, and returning. The problem with this concept was that the elaborate set-up that was created to launch the rocket into space from earth was not easily redone on the moon. As the Soviets continued to work on the "one ship concept," their American counterparts considered new solutions.

The United States saw these problems and realized that it would be extraordinarily difficult to accomplish the "one ship" mission due to the engineering capabilities of the time. Getting out of the traditional paradigm, American engineers created multiple ships that docked and came apart. Hence, the United States landed on the moon and returned to earth, and the Soviets never accomplished the flight.

The Soviets suffered a complete failure to reach the objectives of their original mission, just as decade after decade of school reformers have also failed to reach the objectives of their original mission. If the analogy of "paradigm blindness" holds true (see introduction), the result of our failure to consider new solutions for how schools should operate will also result in perpetual failure. In fact, hasn't that long been the case?

The failure of the Soviet system to fix a perpetual problem with their space program was indicative of a larger failure to seek solutions outside of an existing "answer box." Thus, when new problems arose in the Soviet Union, they were also deemed to be unsolvable, until the empire collapsed. In the United States, a failure to solve the disease that is permeating our public schools will lead to a collapse of all the things this society has been built on. In the twenty-first century, "Life, Liberty and the pursuit of Happiness" are completely intertwined with a quality education.

For a solution to be implemented, a new awareness must be present. The focus of this book is that schools operate under false principles based on false paradigms that have been proven false by our perpetual educational crisis. Unfortunately, virtually all the key decision-makers in our society have missed the core reason why American schools are failing. Today's educational reformers are sure that competition and accountability are missing from the public schools; and therefore, when these concepts are introduced, schools will be fixed. Even if these policy-makers are correct— which they are not—the system will make sure that true competition and true accountability never really take place.

Hence, bad schools are rarely closed down and the real decision-makers—boards of education, superintendents, and elected officials—are unlikely to ever be evaluated and held publicly accountable for failing schools. Furthermore, the accountability measures they are using, the standardized test, have the potential to destroy the creative and the good presently in the system.

The methodology for creating competition and accountability has been the widespread use of standardized tests. As curriculum has been narrowed and instruction has changed to a "passing the

test" mentality, this "testing mania" is causing the institutionaliza-
tion of many of the bad practices that caused the problem in the
first place. The students who think "out of the box"—the mind that
has been the creative thinker that has been at the core of America's
genius—will not be produced by schools that specialize in rote
memorization based on success on standardized testing.

America's schools are failing because they displease their consumer. When their consumers are seven- or ten-year-old children,
they just shut down and refuse to comply. When the consumers
pass the age of sixteen, they run away by the tens of thousands.
Other students—the ones from the upper-middle-class schools—
comply with occasional mistreatment, frequent use of bad pedagogy, curriculum that is focused on lower-order thinking skills, and a
justice system based on "shut your mouth" and "go along to get
along."

It has become apparent that the problems in the world of
American public education have become systemic and chronic. The
root cause behind the fact that solutions have been elusive is our
thinking process. We are simply not well equipped to look at why
past solutions have failed to change the negative dynamic of public
schooling. If we want to solve the problems of the public schools
once and for all, we have to look at why our past attempts have
repeatedly failed.

Today we live in a society in which we employ negative practices rather than solve problems. We are continually looking to who
can be blamed for the creation of the problem. We somehow think
finding a villain will make solutions clearer. Today's wave of educational bashing has been centered on teacher accountability
scores. For the present reformers, the problem must be the teachers.
Or if not teachers alone, then perhaps the principals are also the
problem. One thing is certain for educational reformers: without a
villain, no solution will be found.

What has made matters worse is that those who enact solutions to societal problems rarely if ever engage in a legitimate audit to determine if their interventions have worked. Given these factors, we are caught in a perpetual state of problem solving. Failed solutions have become a permanent condition of modern life. Perhaps no institution has suffered more from the "blame-broken fix" continuum than the American public school.

Federal interventions, such as Goals 2000, No Child Left Behind, and Race to the Top, have left Americans desirous of real solutions to the problems of the American public schools.

Today a business model based on accountability has been employed to fix the problems of the public schools. The latest waive of accountability features teachers being held accountable for student performance on standardized tests. This will not fix the public schools, and it will be most certainly the latest failure in a chain of failures.

The authors respect teachers, administrators, government officials, board members, and others who are involved in the world of education. However, each group in its own way has inadvertently made the problems of the public schools worse. While each wants what's better for children, each has offered solutions that simply fail, have failed, and will fail for the very same reason; they have misunderstood the real problem with the American public schools.

The American public schools are "Screwed-Up." But they are fixable and their better days can be now. However, if the reformers keep missing the point, try to change schools without changing foundation beliefs, and continue to fail to meet the needs of the children that walk through the schoolhouse door, failure will be the outcome for too many children, resulting in too many wasted lives. We offer a solution to "Screwed-Up."

Chapter One

Screwed-Up by the Wrong Paradigms: The Conflicting Purposes of Public Schools

RIDING THE TIGER

As American parents, grandparents, and children have pleaded for better public schools, federal and local governments have responded with a multitude of reforms. However, one does not have to be a great prophet to realize that the present educational reform movement in the United States is failing and will continue to fall short of its goals and purposes if things don't change. In fact, over the decades, virtually every effort to improve the American public schools has not met its goals. This constant chain of educational reform has been riddled with political agendas and flawed remedies, leading to few improvements.

Through the years, reformers have found their efforts to improve the public schools were analogous to the experience one would have in riding a tiger. Once the reform effort began to be implemented, the reformers quickly found that they had little to no control over the directions they were headed—nor was getting off the tiger's back the best or easiest of ideas/tasks. Failure to recognize the fundamental problems in many school reform efforts has left the public schools journeying down the wrong road in search of answers for decades.

Present reformers try hard and truly believe that their vigorous effort to alter the situation will be different from past attempts. But as time goes on, policy-makers and educators also will find themselves on the back of a tiger, taking them in directions they do not want to go—and will be unwilling to admit they can't get off or change direction.

Solutions have focused on the symptoms of the broken public schools rather than the disease causing the problems. Additionally, the series of interventions enacted by reformers failed to perceive that larger bureaucratic systems invariably revert back to how they operated prior to a reform. As a result of the broken approach to education reform, failure was and is all but guaranteed in the future, unless a new method is used.

So, as educational reform efforts have strung together failure after failure, we can assume logically that the next generation of education policy-makers at all levels should closely consider the foundation problems that lessened success in prior reform movements. However, even logic has not been employed as the creators of the last two major federal programs in education—No Child Left Behind and the Race to the Top—have designed their reform intervention with little to no idea as to why prior efforts at reform fell short and of how to overcome the real problems.

THE PROBLEM

So what is wrong? Why are the public schools so difficult to fix? The simple answer is that all attempts at reforming the public school have ignored the core problem—a dilemma we can figure out once we leave the "answer box" that our brain has created. Our "answer box" is the artificial parameters we create within our brain in which all possible solutions can be found.

The main resource we use for all problem-solving is our brain, which has developed an elegant system for making sense of the world based on the concept that all solutions can be found within the "answer box" that we have developed throughout our lives. Our life experiences, intellectual capacities, and the filters through which we see the world have helped to create our answer box.

The more intelligent and successful the individual is, the more he or she has come to rely on an internal answer box. The problem lies in the subjective nature by which we view our life experiences and the filters we have developed to make sense of the world. As a result, the best educators, politicians, and academicians have continually applied solutions to the problems of the public schools while never identifying the real issues. Invariably, reformers have treated the symptoms, as the disease continues to flourish and affect the system.

The core problem of the American public schools is that for an overwhelming percentage of students, schools are places where joy and emotional fulfillment are nearly absent. Reformers treating the symptom of dropouts and poor test performance have not identified the absence of student happiness and satisfaction as the real "disease" permeating the system. Additionally, the concept of treating children with love as a main ingredient for academic success is an alien concept in most schoolhouses of America.

Remarkably, the educational reform movement has rarely considered that kids who do not like being in school, are afraid in school, are bored in school, or do not feel important in school *will* ultimately reject the product being offered. Former U.S. secretary of education Margaret Spelling claimed that the national graduation rate was 66 percent; but she also stated that that figure is an exaggeration based on the way states compile their data.

According to "The Schott 50 State Report on Public Education and Black Males" (2010), only 25 percent of African American men from New York State and 47 percent nationally graduate from high school, showing that the percentage of American students who reject their education in one form or another is staggering. Numerous books and studies on the issue have discussed what is wrong in our schools. But even the researchers who manage to uncover the reasons or causes of the emotional disease afflicting schools tend to obscure—or surround—the truth in a morass of other information that inherently serves to become disinformation and confusion.

American schools have two main groups of students: the first has enough home support and/or self-reliance to see themselves through to the high school graduation ceremony. The second group is unable to learn and benefit from education for personal, family, or community reasons and do poorly, drop out, or just fail to learn and graduate from high school. The fractured approach to school reform has had serious negative outcomes in American society.

Educational reform efforts have done little to heal the wounds that emotionally troubled students bring into their schooling. Without an appropriate intervention in school, these emotionally troubled students have an extraordinarily difficult time reaching successful life outcomes. Even students who have arrived at the schoolhouse door emotionally healthy and proceed successfully to graduation, invariably, can recite a long list of complaints they have with their education and treatment at school.

Most commonly, when customers of a business are unhappy with a product or service, they will not complain; instead, they simply do not come back or "buy" it again. In schools, when students want to complain about their treatment, courses of study, boring pedagogy, lack of rigor (for lower-tracked students), or the overwhelming amounts of work (for some upper-tracked students), the system has no mechanism for hearing their voices, examining their complaints and concerns, and making positive change.

Because the public schools do not have a real feedback system, schools are allowed to operate in violation of the basic needs of children. Students themselves, in fact, have gone online, using Internet sites such as RateMyTeachers.com, which has recorded 11 million reviews by students of teachers in their schools. But who pays any attention to what students think or say, even when reading their comments, critiques, and suggestions teacher-by-teacher online?

All school reforms will thus fail until reformers recognize that what they are dealing with, at the basic level, is an unhappy customer. Students are consumers and participants who need to be loved and treated with kindness. Today's effort at school reform has substituted an arbitrary assessment for that love, using accountability instead of caring. Reforms have focused on a narrow test-preparation model and test outcomes—at the cost of an exciting, meaningful learning experience.

But we are on to our next reform movement, dubbed by the Obama administration the Race to the Top. Given that the cure has ignored the disease—and again attempted to treat the symptoms—we might better have called it, Race to the Flop (or perhaps Flop to the Top). The administration has climbed onto the back of the tiger, the movement is off and running, the direction will be determined by the tiger, and what is worse, the administration won't get off the tiger's back for fear of being devoured.

Reformers hold many news conferences when they usher in their latest and greatest reform. These same individuals disappear when the reform has failed. No one held a news conference in 2000 when Goals 2000 failed on every level, while the 1989 news conference to introduce the movement was well attended and quite optimistic.

THIS BOOK: PURPOSES AND MEANS

This book advocates treating students the way we want our own children and grandchildren to be treated. Reform movements must embrace love, fun, meaningfulness, appropriate rigor, feedback, community, positive relationships, and exciting activities for all children. Presidents and U.S. secretaries of education want no less for their own children. These are good people; and ultimately if they understood the core problems, they would advocate for all our children as well.

WHY GOOD PEOPLE MAKE BAD CHOICES

Case 1—A doctor working on his garden at home gets an emergency call that he is needed at the hospital immediately. He arrives at the hospital and finds a patient about to give birth to her child. An attending nurse stops the procedure as the doctor begins to deliver the baby without washing his hands that are clearly sullied by his prior activities. Of course, this type of situation is unheard of in today's medical world. The accepted core principle of the medical field is for doctors to wash their hands in an antiseptic solution prior to delivering a baby. However, in 1847, when medical professor Ignac Semmelweis presented evidence to his colleagues that washing hands in a chlorine solution prior to delivering a baby would save lives, he was rebuffed.

Case 2—When George Washington came down with a severe throat infection, doctors were called. The first doctor initiated the "best practice" of the day: he placed leeches on Washington to remove the bad blood. The second doctor who examined Washington decided that more was better and furthered the "best practice" with more leeches and more blood removal. A few hours later Washington's condition took a turn for the worse. A third doctor was called to help with the situation. He also decided that Washington needed immediate treatment—and took more blood. Washington died shortly after these medical interventions.

Case 3—In 1616, Italian astronomer Galileo was called to Rome to speak to church officials regarding his advocacy of the "Copernican System," which stated that the earth revolved around the sun.

The church hierarchy forbad him from teaching or advocating the theory as it constituted heresy. In 1632 Galileo mentioned the theory in his writings and was placed on trial in 1633, that trial resulting in his placement in "enforced residency." It wasn't until 1992 that the church admitted that the treatment of Galileo was uncalled for and that he was in fact correct.

Case 4—Futurist Joel Barker tells the story of a man who goes for a drive on a beautiful Sunday on a mountain road. As he approaches a bend in the road, a car comes around the corner, being driven wildly. And the woman inside the car is screaming, "Pig!" Next, the woman's car swerves at the last minute back into her lane and avoids an accident. The man is appalled. Not only does she almost kill him, but she also insults him on top of it. He leans out his window and yells, "Hog!"—satisfied he has evened the score. He proceeds to drive around the bend and hits a group of pigs in the road. "Pig!" was a warning, not an insult.

These four case stories are examples of the way the human brain operates. Each day, we are inundated with information; and as a result, we need methods to sort the important from the trivial, the reasonable from the absurd, and the reality from the fantasy. The tools that we have created to filter information have been described by scientists as *paradigms*: a means to process new information so that it is understandable, useable, and acceptable to us.

However, as the examples above have illustrated, using paradigms to interpret information can also lead us down the wrong path. In fact, a diagnosed condition exists that scientists call "paradigm blindness." The situation was named to describe a condition when scientific researchers came up with an outcome that was so unexpected and so far from the norm that the scientists were simply blind to their own findings.

In the eighteenth century, removing blood from sick individuals made the patients even sicker. However, the negative outcome of blood letting was so far from the accepted norm that doctors never considered the possibility that the practice was harmful. Since physicians in the first part of the nineteenth century had not heard of bacteria, the concept of washing their hands before delivering a baby, or performing other medical procedures, made no logical sense.

Church leaders in the sixteenth and seventeenth centuries considered the concept that the earth was the center of our universe as evidence that God had chosen us and our planet as special. Furthermore, if the church hierarchy was wrong about the planets and sun, about what else might they also be confused? Exploring the concept that the church could be wrong was not allowed; and anyone who questioned church doctrine on an important level had to be silenced.

Our brain can thus use paradigms to identify when we are insulted or complimented. In addition to spoken words, we use body language, voice inflection, and face reading to interpret such messages. When the man driving on a beautiful Sunday heard the word "Pig," he heard an insult—but he needed to hear a warning! When he misinterpreted the message, based on how his brain filtered the information, he put himself and others at great risk.

Good people make bad choices when they can't get past their paradigms in considering chronic problems. The condition affects doctors, lawyers, politicians, educators, academicians—and in fact, all of us. Because of paradigm blindness, we have not seen the real problem affecting schools. However, this myopia has not stopped us from going to reform movement after reform movement, failure after failure, without finding a solution. Additionally, as is the norm with human beings, when the ideas and implementation of reform initiatives are questioned, the reformers often hear an insult.

Furthermore, reformers take extraordinary measures to make it appear that the change is working. For example, in many states, the passing rate for elementary or middle school students on standardized assessments has been set at a variable cut point. As a result, the passing score one year is likely to be a different score the following year. With changing cut points for passing, the reformers can manipulate outcomes to determine success. Therefore, at any time, a case can be made that students are doing better as a result of the reform effort.

Because good people make bad choices, schools will continue to deliver a substandard product unless we wash our hands, stop bleeding our children, learn to differentiate an insult from a warning, and realize which way the world is turning.

BETTER AT WHAT?

One of the numerous problems educational reformers confront is a lack of clarity as to the purpose of schooling. The questions of what we want to be better at—and accomplish—have been different and changing, based on the generation and the group asking the questions. This confusion is not new, as the purpose of education has been debated since the inception of the public school system in the nineteenth century. Today, the dominant theories regarding the purpose of schools are related to our economic standing and general security in an increasingly complex world.

The argument since *A Nation at Risk* was published in 1983 is that without better public schools, our very existence as a nation is at risk. The dominant arguments for improving the public schools are inherently fear based. If we do not fix the schools, we will be poorer and at greater risk of domination (economically and even politically) by other countries. The unspoken truth is that the national movement toward administering standardized tests is an outgrowth of the belief that the public schools, left on their own, will not measure up to the task of protecting and expanding America.

A major problem with many multigenerational school reform movements is that they were built on this foundation of fear. American school reformers are continually running away from some great threat that may or may not imminently affect our way of life. When the brain of human beings goes into a fear-based, near-panic response, physiological changes take place. For example, our vision becomes more peripheral to spot threats from all sides. As we see better to the sides, our ability to focus on any task *in front of us* declines. Fear-based solutions have a greater tendency toward urgent, knee-jerk reactions and answers that provide an extremely poor solution for considering unintended side effects of the intervention. The fear-based reform movement has left us worse off, including the intervention's side effects (unanticipated results) that have often had a deleterious impact on the children who have been subjects of the strategy.

The reform movements, based on economic and political security in the future, have little to no measurement in today's world. Will better test scores on a fourth-grade ELA (English Language Arts assessment) really protect us from the nuclear proliferation that may occur in Iran? Will better scores on the eighth-grade assessment in math help us to stop the disastrous trade imbalance with China? What we can measure—the quality of schooling, the ability of graduates, and the graduation rate—indicates a continuing disaster.

We still have a student dropout epidemic, and even our best students leave school with horror stories of treatment at the hands of adults and peers. Our top students often indicate they succeed in spite of their schooling. The weak instructional pedagogy and the uneven curriculum of their schools have left them desirous and curious of what a quality education might have been like. So as educational reformers promise that their efforts will make our schools better, the key question really is— *better at what?*

IGNORING THAT STUDENTS ARE ACTUALLY CHILDREN—FAILED REFORM BECOMES THE NORM

In the flurry of reform in America's schools, a myriad of education reforms have been enacted. Even though politicians and educational experts strive to institutionalize change and improve our nation's schools, a staggering program of mediocrity continues to weaken our educational institutions. Observing these failures, few researchers have recognized that America's students have been systematically overlooked and disconnected from the school restructuring and reform process itself.

Decision-makers have come to view students' dissatisfaction with—and failure in—school systems as the normal state of affairs. This attitude has allowed schools to operate in violation of many of the basic social and psychological needs of human beings. As a consequence, many students are rejecting their education altogether, or at best, only doing substandard work to get by.

The inherent problem of American schools has been that all efforts for reform have been based on erroneous foundation principles. Intuitively, we can all recognize when we have embarked on a journey traveling down the wrong road that never gets us to our desired destination. Hence, America's schools are caught in a never-ending cycle of failed reform followed by more and "better" failed reform. Until the concepts of recognizing and institutionalizing the human needs of children are at the center of school reform, the reform movements will continue to be lost, traveling down the wrong road to a place called "failure."

CONCEPTS

Following World War II, W. E. Deming attempted to introduce principles of quality management into the American auto industry. The American carmakers, which were dominating world sales at the time, dismissed his concepts. However, the Japanese auto companies embraced Deming's concepts; and by the turn of the century these carmakers had institutionalized the correlation between quality and a Japanese car. Accordingly, Lexus and Infinity are today the Cadillac and Lincoln of yesterday. William Glasser believes America's schools must emulate W. E. Deming's work with industry to achieve a quality education for all students. As Glasser (1990) states:

> There are remarkable parallels between the American manufacturers who ignored Deming when he suggested that they make quality their number one priority after World War II and the school managers who seem unconcerned that only a few students in any secondary school do what we—or even they—would call high-quality work. Like the automakers in the Seventies, who concentrated on building a lot of low-quality, high-profit cars and who might have gone bankrupt if competition had been unrestricted, our schools have been primarily concerned with trying to get some students to do enough work to reach the low standard of quality required for high school graduation. (p. 427)

As we have entered the third century of the American public schools, our paradigms regarding their purpose have become part of the problem. As a society, we have never reached general agreement about what we want and expect from our schools; and as such, we have become infected with faddism based on whatever the "latest and greatest" concept happens to be. In the 1950s and 1960s, we criticized our public schools (1) for our soldiers' (as POWs) failure to resist brain washing in the Korean War, (2) for being behind in the space race after the Russians launched *Sputnik* in 1957, and (3) for having young people protesting the government and acting badly during the Vietnam War.

As a result, the seeming inability of the schools to teach good character, appropriate behavior, and science became key elements in the educational reform dialogue during those decades. Following the 1983 publication of *A Nation at Risk*, the general consensus became that our very survival as a nation was threatened because our public schools were not producing a product that would allow us to compete on the world stage.

For the most part, this assertion has been interpreted now as our being able to compete successfully in an economic model designed to maintain our dominance in lifestyle in comparison to the rest of the world. As a result, we have been on a mission to improve our schools so as to save our lifestyle.

Virtually all the reform efforts in the latter part of the twentieth century, and the first decade of the new century, have failed and will continue to fail for many of the same reasons. Reformers constantly look at students as pieces of clay that can be molded to fit whatever pattern society decides is desirable, necessary, and urgent—at the moment. Little to no consideration is given to the belief that young people have their own thoughts, desires, needs, feelings, and wishes regarding their schooling and their future lives.

Additionally, as schools are usually overseen by elected boards of education that are traditionally stocked with parents, the disconnect between what many parents want for their children and the everyday organizational life of students in the schoolhouse seems extraordinarily confusing. This lack of clarity becomes more understandable when one considers that the parents and other citizens who are in positions of decision-makers are themselves suffering from the same paradigm blindness as the educators and politicians entrusted with decision-making in schools.

In the case of schools, the "blinding paradigms" have often become the foundation beliefs. That being true, students must learn responsibility to (1) sit still, (2) obey authority, (3) work hard even when it is not fun, (4) operate isolated from other students, (5) compete with other students for higher grades, (6) please the teacher, (7) play the game, (8) desire high grades regardless of how much learning takes place, (9) work in an environment that is not pleasing, (10) survive in a world where they are physically threatened, (11) live in a world where students may be ridiculed by peer and adult alike, and (12) move into a world that makes them unhappy and just feel bad!!!

These foundation beliefs may work for a piece of clay, but they will never be effective for a young person. So educational reformers can advocate the use of accountability testing—embarrassing schools by publicizing outcome data that reveal low test scores—set goals, create charter schools, and more. None of these processes has worked, and none of them will work because schools operate in violation of people's basic human needs. In short, we treat children in ways that we would not or should not treat adults.

Then, as a society, we wonder why the results of our public schools, decade after decade, are substandard and disappointing. Regarding schools, educators, politicians, and parents are the twenty-first-century equivalent to George Washington's doctors. We are draining the lifeblood from the ones whom we love, and then are puzzled why things never improve.

President George H. W. Bush endorsed Goals 2000 (1989), stating that the students of the United States would be first in the world in math and science by the year 2000. The deadline came and went, but little to no dialogue occurred about what happened or failed. Why should it? We as a society were on to yet another new reform effort that ultimately failed as well.

THE CASE FOR STUDENT INVOLVEMENT IN SCHOOL DECISIONS

To maintain discipline with unhappy consumers (students), educators (with parental backing) have created elaborate compliance systems based on stimuli-response theory. The concept is that if we evaluate and then punish students enough, they will do what we want. But the evidence is overwhelming, e.g., that students will do what is most satisfying to them at the moment has been completely ignored. Abraham Maslow said that anyone who believed that the behavior of young people could be changed by using stimuli-response techniques has never been a parent. Since the compliance systems have failed, in 1990 William Glasser stated that over 85 percent of American students were committing educational suicide. Glasser wrote in *The Quality School*:

> Students have a good idea of what parts of their schooling are of high quality. . . almost none find anything of high quality in regular classes. All except a very few admit that, while they believe that they are capable of doing high-quality work in class, they have never actually done any and have no plans to do any in the future. (1990, p. 426)

In a 1996 study, students were asked to rate their treatment by adults and their educational satisfaction at five middle- and upper-middle-class high schools in New York State. Fewer than 15 percent rated their treatment as "excellent," and just 29 percent reported they were "very satisfied" with their education. More than a third of students polled reported that the treatment they received from adults in their school was fair to poor (Shear, 1996). Compounding these troubling results is that the majority of students surveyed were from schools in wealthier communities that would be considered highly successful in comparison to other American high schools.

Thus, the study indicated that even students at the highest performing schools wanted to be part of the dialogue of school reform and operation. When asked if schools would get better if students were included in the decision-making process, 89 percent of respondents indicated that schools would improve to some degree, and 38 percent of those polled indicated that the improvement would be great (Shear, 1996).

In 1970, Silberman wrote that the failure to address students' educational concerns was not new; rather the same students' displeasures with schools have existed for more than a century. Nearly four decades ago, Annie Stein (1971) expressed the needs of students this way: "They want a better education, a more relevant curriculum, and some respect for their constitutional and human rights" (p. 177). Sonya Nieto (1994) stated, "The voices of students are rarely heard in the debates about school failure and success, and the perspectives of students from disempowered and dominated communities are even more invisible" (p. 396). Furthermore, Nieto wrote,

> I am instead suggesting that if we believe schools must provide an equal and quality education for all, students need to be included in the dialogue, and that their views, just as those of others, should be problematized and used to reflect critically on school reform. (p. 396)

Nieto is joined by educators, researchers, and academicians in redefining students' roles in schools. Alfie Kohn (1993) argues, "In classrooms where students can make choices about learning . . . the need for punishments or rewards declines sharply" (cited in Brandt, 1995, p. 13). Anne Wescott Dodd (1995) implores teachers to "invite students to help you solve classroom problems" (p. 17). And in *The Case for Constructivist Classrooms*, J. G. Brooks and M. G. Brooks (1993) present a rationale for attaining students' inclusion in the dialogue of education. The authors state, "One of the crucial principles of constructivism is the seeking and valuing of students' points of view" (p. 17). Pierce and Stein (1995), in performing an educational assessment, argued for students' full participation in the process. They explained, "To promote equity in educational assessment, different stakeholders, such as testers, teachers, administrators, parents, and students should be able to contribute to the test development process" (p. 62).

Today, for the most part, students' *involvement* and *participation* in education are rejected; in fact, their role is not even discussed. Students have been considered unable to understand the pedagogy of education or to offer meaningful solutions to the problems of schools. In summarizing the way students have been excluded from the educational dialogue, Soo Hoo (1993) explains, "We listen to outside experts to inform us, and consequently, we overlook the treasure in our very own backyards: our students" (p. 391). Additionally, Soo Hoo discovered that students were far more capable of sophisticated judgments regarding their education than previously thought. She found that "students placed in positions of responsibility and shared authority could actively investigate what was working and not working for them as learners" (p. 386).

Sonya Nieto (1994) made the same discovery after working closely with students:

> The insights provided by the students were far richer than we had first thought. Although we expected numerous criticisms of schools and some concrete suggestions, we were surprised at the depth of awareness and analysis the students shared with us. (p. 397)

A 1992 study by the Institute for Education in Transformation at the Claremont Graduate School claimed that the reform movement's failure to understand what students were experiencing may have been counterproductive to the improvement of schools (Weeres & Poplin, 1992). The evidence is thus abundant: as the American school system continues to institute new reform efforts, based on old foundation beliefs, little will change.

ASKING THE STUDENTS

A fair question to ask is, *What do students want?* What should be the appropriate foundation values of schools and what paradigms should be used for creating the successful public schools of the twenty-first century?

Any consideration of what students prefer should feature the voice of students. *Voices from the Inside* (Weeres & Poplin, 1992) chronicled a year of researchers living in four schools in California. Students commenting on their lives in school made the following statements:

> I'm not that safe in school (middle school student; p. 15).

> My perfect school would have everything except violence things (elementary school student; p. 16).

> Not all teachers are doing more good than harm . . . some teachers don't care, which is scary because of the influence of teachers (middle school student; p. 19).

> In school, I don't like unfriendly people and being friendless (elementary school student; p. 20).

> My first-period teacher seems so malevolent and shows no clemency towards us (high school student; p. 20).

The perfect school would be where . . . all students have a desk (high school student; p. 35).

Basically, they talk and we listen (high school student; p. 36).

My teacher has no regard for me as a person, but just sees me as another student to be stereotyped (high school student; p. 36).

Our future is being thrown away (high school student; p. 37).

And thus, evidence of the students' condition has been around for many years. However, the foundation principles of schooling have not changed. Today's effort at school reform features the attempt to manipulate student outcomes through external means, such as setting higher standards and performing more accountability testing without consulting with the clients, the students themselves. The effort is foolish and will fail to make significant improvement in the public schools. However, a good thing about being a school reformer is that when these efforts do not succeed, policy-makers can either go away, claim the initiative was not followed correctly, or even blame the students (victims).

In any case, leaders never have to own up to the reality that the reform efforts were based on erroneous foundation beliefs. Additionally, the idea that publicly backed charter schools will help only ignores that the problems of schooling are systemic and must be solved on a systemic basis. Removing a few children from one system and putting them into another, for example—with the hope that they will get a better education—will neither change the totality of the system nor benefit most students.

Schools are not systems just for transmitting information or preparing students for college or the business world. Schools must teach students living in a fragmented world how to care for each other. The United States is a multicultural country, inhabited by peoples from all over the world. The best hope for our survival, internal peace, and prosperity is the public schools. In the public schools, children of the world come together to become Americans.

Anything that erodes the ability of the public schools to improve and prosper also threatens the ability of the United States to survive as a nation. The future of the United States, as we know it, is to a large degree based on having successful public schools. Great public schools will only become a reality when new foundation principles include student involvement and participation in issues of schooling. A satisfied consumer is the new foundation belief of twenty-first-century schools and our best "product."

THE HIDDEN DANGER OF VIOLATING STUDENTS' HUMAN NEEDS

The most telling quote from *Voices from the Inside* is "This place hurts my spirit" (high school student; 1992, p. 11). We have systematically broken down students' will until they and their parents have come to expect that the quality of schools will range from mediocre to bad. When schools operate without receiving feedback from the consumer, the hidden agenda is that abuse can and often does become standard operating procedure, as a co-teacher explained to Shear:

> I asked the principal to be removed from her class. I mean everyone knows the way she treats kids. After she abuses a 2nd grader, I move over to the child to make sure the child is OK. The principal takes her on 3 or 4 times a year, but what can you do with a tenured teacher? The principal took on a lot of difficult teachers, and that is probably why she was forced to retire.

Human beings need to provide and receive feedback as part of the processes of life. In *Organizations*, Gibson, Ivancevich, and Donnelly (1979) reported that zero feedback engenders doubt and hostilities toward the senders of the communication—and the inability to discuss experiences will result in a decline in productivity and quality, increased absenteeism, and/or conflict.

The outcomes associated with a lack of communication are characteristic of student performance in America's public schools. The disenfranchisement of students has made them angry; and as unhappy consumers, students then show their displeasure with their absenteeism, class cutting, inattention, and an incredibly high national drop-out rate. However, the process of running schools—absent consumer feedback—has ultimately created a system that operates on a level of mediocrity or worse. Research indicates that the very act of asking students their opinion can improve the students' attitudes toward their schooling (Kohn, 1993).

Human beings model the behaviors that they witness. In a society that is increasingly concerned with bullying behavior in schools, for example, consideration is rarely given to the way in which adults treat children. The hidden danger of schools that are allowed to operate in violation of basic human needs is that they set the stage for creating a generation that also operates in violation of basic human needs. The question our society should answer is, *How much of the negative culture that permeates our society could have been prevented by healthy schools?*

Unfortunately, we will never know what would or could have happened if we had taken another road. But the time has come to replace the wrong paradigms regarding the purpose of schools with the right ones. We need to find out what positive outcomes society will experience when the human rights and feelings of children are honored and nurtured in our public schools.

THE RIGHT PARADIGMS/THE TRUE PURPOSES OF SCHOOLS

What do we want for our children? And our grandchildren? What do we hope our society will look like? How do we want the next generation to approach life, each other, and our planet? The true purpose of schools—the goals we need to have for our children—must be based on these questions. We clearly should stop trying to improve school outcomes from a position of fear. We must reform schools from a place of love—we are dealing with our children and we know what we want for them.

We are not running our schools in accordance with what we want for our children; this is a result of paradigm blindness. We must stop looking at schooling as an operation based on creating a "better tomorrow" and start seeing it as an important social reality for the upbringing of our children today.

The true purpose of schooling must be consistent with the concepts of love and must create schools that are places of love, warmth, discovery, companionship, joy, fun, and meaningfulness. The fact that today's schools do not know how to organize along these lines is not a deal breaker going forward. Moreover, once reformers recognize that the paradigms that guide our schools have been wrong, new solutions will follow quickly.

NEW PARADIGMS

Children need to be told that they are loved, and children need to feel that they are loved. Love means we take care of each other, that we do the right thing by and for each other. When we are loved, we understand that the other person wants what is best for us. New paradigm: *Schools are loving places*.

Children need to believe that schools are warm places, *warm* being defined as caring, safe, and secure. They want to know that people in the schoolhouse care about them as important people. Children need to see warmth, security, and caring modeled. Schools should be designed to facilitate warmth. New paradigm: *Schools are warm places.*

Children love to learn. At the heart of learning is discovery, as it opens the mind and excites the spirit with the possibility of new ideas. Schools should thus be centers of discovery. Lessons need to be built around the concept of discovery and not just around memorizing facts and figures and test preparation. New paradigm: *Schools are places where learning is based on discovery.*

Since human beings are communal creatures, solitary, isolating practices are hurtful and harmful to the soul. Children who do not feel comfortable and may be different must be welcomed and included in the group. Today we have a society in which differences are bad, as being different can get students into a whole lot of trouble in school. As one key adult explained, "Of course I was picked on; I was just a fat, band kid" (Bill Clinton, forty-second president of the United States). New paradigm: *Schools are places of community where no one is excluded and differences are celebrated.*

We want our children to live in a state of joy, getting up excited about the day, confident that good things are coming. Joy is the home of smiling faces and warm embraces. Joy is going to a place where children know that they are safe, valued, and welcome. New paradigm: *Schools are joyful places.*

Who doesn't want to have fun? We hope life will be fun; we want learning to be fun, and we want every moment of every day to be fun. Lessons should be fun-based. Hallways should be fun-based. Classrooms should be fun. New paradigm: *Schools are places of real fun.*

One of the wrong concepts regarding schools is that kids have to be forced to learn. The truth is human beings love to learn. But the learning must be meaningful and relevant to life by answering important questions and making important connections. New paradigm: *Schools are places where meaningful things are learned and meaningful activities take place.*

THE PURPOSE OF THE PUBLIC SCHOOLS

We want our children to be able to learn fundamental information about our world and to be able to apply what they have learned in the pursuit of solving problems facing the human race. Children, we believe, want to grow up to have a society in which people work hard, pursue meaningful goals for self-betterment, and seek the betterment of our world. We thus seek for our children to learn to evolve their personal intellect into wisdom.

We hope our children will have a great life in school. And after their formal education has been completed, they will live in a joyful state of mind. We seek to have our public schools produce well-educated people who are able to laugh and cry, to have empathy for others, and to leave our world better than they found it. We seek for our children to create the kind of world that we have dreamed about, written about, and constantly fallen short of achieving. We want our public schools to be the facilitator for these critical developments and more.

SUMMARY

The effort to fix the broken public school system has reached a fever pitch over the last decade. However, these new reforms will fail as surely as the previous efforts that have been attempted. The conventional approach in our society is to attack the reformers, educators, and government officials for their lack of foresight once it's too late and a reform effort has failed. The better approach is to applaud those who are trying to make things better for our children. The various groups that are seeking to institute a better public school system simply need some clarification to enable their efforts to succeed. As we explore what children really need in school, a new approach will surely emerge from the very fine people who are working on behalf of our children.

Accordingly, we shall explore how educators can be empowered to ensure that those who have dedicated their lives to helping children are a positive energy force for foundation level change. Hence, this book will also explore how the real leaders of schools, the parents, can be better enlightened to a new paradigm of schooling. The parents of a community are the real functioning board of education and parent teacher association (PTA). Their inability to fix their schools has been based on false paradigms that they have been handed by the system and prior generations. The parents and public can best lead an appropriate re-correction of the foundation of schooling.

Government intervention has been misguided as it has tried to evaluate schools using an accountability model that really has never held educators accountable. The role of government in making our public schools great cannot and should not be underestimated. However, a positive new role for government will be articulated in this book, as we can look forward to a renewed partnership between government and the public schools on behalf of children.

We will introduce new solutions built around new paradigms in the following chapters. Once schools are aligned with meeting the needs of children, we will affirm a new paradigm for a new century. We will break the paradigm of looking for someone to blame and instead will seek to create a fertile ground for solutions for the many who are now stuck in a revolving cycle of missed opportunities and poor performance.

This book thus introduces solutions built around a new model, wherein schools are aligned with the needs of children in the hands of exciting teachers in schools led by creative principals. We move from looking for someone to blame to seeking creative grounds for breaking the cycle of failure. In the chapters to follow, we introduce the Four A's of improved practice: agenda, actors, actions, and accomplishments (see figure 1) with the following characteristics.

- *Agendas of Change*, creating joyful, loving schools for all children;
- *Agents/Actors of New Paradigms*, including teachers, school leaders, and parents who ask students about their needs and then participate in making schools exciting, happy places for students and the adults who care for them;
- *Actions that Matter*, as schools become reformed and classrooms are centers of joy and learning; and
- *Accomplishments of Change*, for as schools change, the feelings and beliefs (affect) of participants will also change.

Thus, this book looks at what will change, in the hands of adults who affect the students, making real change work. The book will explore the concept that the people who operate the educational system must take the lead in changing a failed system entrenched in mediocrity. We will consider what it means to give students what they need for a successful school experience. Advice will be offered as to what educators must do with newfound empowerment. The writing will offer a guide for parents and boards of education to improve their roles as the most important educators in the lives of their children.

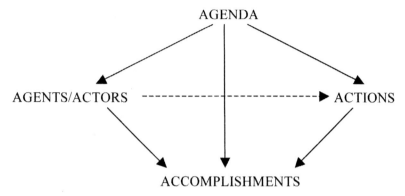

Figure 1.1.   Four A's—Framework of Book

We will offer appropriate actions and a new important role for government to lead in the introduction of better school practices, and we will explore the economic funding and disparity regarding American education's attempts to meet the needs of children. Finally, we will explore what new and successful school practices will mean to our country and world.

Chapter Two

Screwed-Up, by Not Realizing: What Do Students Want? What Do Students Need?

TRUST AND HYPOCRISY

Young people entrust their lives—and their futures—to adults, hoping that grownups will guide them onto the right path; and kids often take the adults at their word. In a literal sense, students want adults to get it right. Further, children hope that adults can create a foundation for their education and lives based on correct principles, not erroneous assumptions. And adults should believe in, and have faith in, their children—assuming that young people can be trusted to do what's best for themselves, and not simply to "do what they are told."

As we discussed in the introduction, the heart of the matter is how teachers and school leaders can create and maintain joy and high emotional fulfillment for students, while teaching them lessons and helping them to learn. This chapter looks at the children: their needs and growth, based on the way schools are organized and run.

FRAMEWORK FOR CHAPTER 2

Let's start with an analogy: Business schools have taught the management concept of Theory X and Theory Y for several decades (McGregor Burns, 1961) as a way of distinguishing one type of manager and "management style" from another. Theory X managers, according to McGregor Burns, believe that workers (employees) are inherently lazy, are unwilling to assume job responsibilities, and are undisciplined. This "factory model" assumes that workers do not want to perform their job at a higher level because of unpleasant working conditions and few rewards for higher performance. As a result, proponents of Theory X assume that workers must be externally compelled to perform their jobs by leaders who are untrusting, direct, controlling, and autocratic.

In contrast, Theory Y management believes that most workers are trustworthy and want to perform well—and thus can be trusted, praised, and respected. When included in the dialogue of management, the employees—and thus the organization—will be more productive.

Unfortunately, many educational decisions made in and about America's public schools are in accordance with the Theory X management model, based on two erroneous foundation beliefs that (1) teachers must be watched and controlled, rather than treated as professionals who in many situations know more than management about their students and subject; and (2) children are rarely eager to be engaged, happy, and open learners, and therefore must be controlled and compelled to do their work.

Rensis Likert (1903–1981), one of the great organizational researchers and theorists, was born in Cheyenne, Wyoming, where his father worked for the Union Pacific Railroad. The younger Likert was an engineering intern. During a railroad strike in 1922,

Rensis Likert noticed the total breakdown of communication between the striking workers and the hostile railroad executives, riveting his attention on the nature of organization behavior.

Likert, like McGregor Burns, looked at the ways those in authority communicate with those who work for and under them, which, Likert found, were "built into" the organization—just as relationships are central to the adult-student relationships in schools. In fact, the very structure of organizations (e.g., schools) reflects the philosophy of the leaders and reinforces this relationship between workers and managers (adults and students). The resulting management "styles" are four, ranging from tightly structured (top down) to those involving the participants and the managers as followers.

Type 1: Exploitive-Authoritative. Decisions and controls are imposed on the subordinates, who must be watched and managed by threats (sound familiar at some schools?) with little or no responsibility or control at the "bottom" of the organization. Little real communication runs up and down, and teamwork is little to none. Perhaps few schools are truly exploitive-authoritative, but students and even teachers are isolated in the most top-down schools: Result—control, control, control.

Type 2: Benevolent-Authoritative. Likert argued that in some organizations, leadership is "a condescending" relationship between "master" and "servant" (administrators, teachers, and students), with little real communication and limited teamwork. Many good principals are considered strong and benevolent, but in full authority; and "good students" keep their mouths shut, "behave themselves," and do what they're told.

Type 3: Consultative-Sharing. Likert noticed that in some organizations, leaders have limited but real trust in their followers, who share ideas and rewards and believe in the goals of the organization. Communication flows upward and downward in the organization; and many participants share in the goal-setting and operation—as ideas flow both vertically and horizontally. Good schools, too, will see extensive consulting, where students, teachers, and school administrators sit together to solve problems—but the principal remains in charge. Likert would approve.

Type 4: Participative–Shared Responsibility. Finally, Likert found that the optimum arrangement in organizations was when and where leaders believed in, and had confidence in, their followers; where organizational goals were set and carried out in collaboration; and where participants played a major role in setting their own goals and pursuing them. In all, Likert focused on three specific causal variables as basic concepts of System 4 management: "the use by the manager of the principles of supportive relationships, his use of group decision making and group methods of supervision, and his high performance goals for the organization" (Likert, 1967, p. 47).

Applications to Students in Schools

The first belief driving the Theory X model, when applied to schools, is that students must be forced to work, learn, and complete tasks because kids deep-down don't care and don't really want to learn. Hence, the belief is that if students are not forced to work, they will not master the material taught and, therefore, will be irreparably harmed. The second misaligned concept is that students, based on their age and immaturity, are unable accurately to ascertain what will and will not work for themselves as learners. As a result, students are disenfranchised from the decision-making process, told what to do, and not given much voice in their own education.

It's no wonder that students have gone off-campus, or online, to use programs like RateMyTeachers.com—where they take some control in assessing their treatment in schools and are able anonymously online to evaluate their teachers. Why not also allow students to evaluate their courses and have a voice in what they want and feel ready to learn, prefer to read, and how they will be taught and evaluated?

UNDERSTANDING THE PROBLEM—FROM THE STUDENTS' PERSPECTIVE

The assumption that students do not want to be in school is based on strong qualitative research. The major discipline problems in most American public high schools are cutting classes and truancy; for as students progress into their teenage years, many of them opt out of school by not complying with attendance regulations. Anyone who visits a school, works in a school, spends time in a school, or knows someone who goes to school is aware that a significant percentage of students are dissatisfied. This unhappiness grows as students progress through the educational system, getting worse as they approach their high school years.

Unfortunately for children and their education, researchers get it wrong when they conclude that students need more external pressure to perform well in school. The qualitative research is observing the right outcome (i.e., that students who do not wish to comply with work and attendance requirements are rampant), while at the same time misinterpreting the cause of their noncompliance. The overwhelming truth is that a lack of student commitment in schools is a result of students being forced to endure poor educational practices, not of students' lack of a desire to learn. Educational researchers are ignoring human nature when they study children. Both researchers and practitioners are "blaming the victims" for the poor outcomes of the product.

Significant consequences result from the second flawed operating concept: the near-total exclusion of students from the decision-making process has allowed the system to operate in an unhealthy manner. Bad practices have become the norm and are seldom discussed and corrected. Additionally, strong research indicates that greater student involvement in their own education would reap a multitude of benefits: instilling joy and emotional growth in the process. The failure to include students in the dialogue of education has resulted in reform efforts that are attempting to solve the "symptoms" of bad schools and not the "disease" causing the problem. As explained twenty years ago,

> Our data strongly suggest that the heretofore identified problems of schooling (lowered achievement, high dropout rates, and problems in the teaching profession) are rather consequences of much deeper and more fundamental problems. Seen through multiethnic students' eyes and the eyes of other participants inside schools, the problems of public education in the U.S. look vastly different than those issues debated by experts, policy makers, academicians and the media. (Weeres & Poplin, 1992, p. 11)

Children do not require more external pressure to perform well in school. Rather, students need three "pillars" of a good education to succeed in school and life: (1) a quality curriculum, (2) intriguing pedagogical practices, and (3) a strong, positive relationship with their peers, faculty, and staff. Lacking any of these fundamental pillars, students will not succeed in accordance with their potential.

Quality Curriculum + Intriguing Pedagogy + Strong Interpersonal Relations = Successful Schools

Lacking any—or all—of these three pillars needed for successful schools, students will often progress in alignment with socioeconomic indicators. What occurs when any of the three pillars is missing is an unpleasant experience: Students from middle- and upper-class homes will often succeed enough to progress to college, while students from lower-class or troubled homes will struggle to graduate from high school. The fact is, students from middle-

and upper-class homes are successfully able to displace pleasure and make it despite their unhappiness. This process is often not true for students coming from disadvantaged backgrounds.

HYPOCRITICAL PRACTICE

Substandard pedagogical practice, poorly constructed curriculum, and/or poor relationships will result in uneven student success. And, in particular, students from impoverished homes have substantially more difficulty in putting off joy to a later time. What is significant is that students, teachers, administrators, parents, academicians, and politicians all agree in principle that school is often boring and difficult to sit through. However, they rarely consider that the schools should change to adapt to human need and become places of joy and excitement.

Perhaps the greatest discouragement for students, as they progress through the school system, is the unspoken feeling of a violation of trust. Young people need to trust that adults are making the right decisions on their behalf. Young people have to believe in their caregivers, including their parents, teachers, administrators, and public officials. The lack of alignment between practice and promise becomes a violation of the human spirit that permeates our society. It would be interesting to consider how this violation of trust has affected society. For the adults of today are the children of yesterday—who endured the same sorry practices based on the same erroneous beliefs that we are observing today.

Children at their core level are vulnerable, and they must trust adults for their very survival. What children have been receiving is food, shelter, and confusion. Long before children know the word *hypocrisy*, they know its meaning. They are told that school is designed to provide them with a better life; however, a better life is not well defined. And everyday school practices require a price, a toll, for children who pay in boredom, subjugation of individual will, and sometimes even fear.

Adults also tell themselves that as a society we teach tolerance. But children who are different in race, background, ability, and needs know that tolerance is not the everyday practice of many of America's public schools. Few of us would want to try, even for one day, being the wrong color, religion, race, weight, or height, or would want to display cross-gender mannerisms in school. Children who are different can tell us all about how well our philosophies of tolerance are operating (not!).

Institutionalized hypocrisy is glaringly found in the school practices of testing and the state and national enforcement of standardized assessment. Children are told they are in school to learn. Politicians, academicians, administrators, teachers, and parents will all trumpet the need for children to learn the curriculum. However, when students fail to learn key concepts, skills, or other measured items sufficiently, they are simply given a failing grade.

The class moves on to the next set of concepts, skills, or items to be measured. The more the subject is sequential, such as math or world languages, the more the student is guaranteed an endless chain of failure. And . . . the class moves on. The concept of mastery learning seems an alien concept in today's schools. Some teachers give students a better grade for redoing work until it is mastered; but these instructors are in the distinct minority. Remediation is mandated by law, but frequently employs second-rate practices that feature redundancy and boredom.

A failing grade doesn't work in the adult world. If employees owe their boss a report and they do not hand it in—or if people do a substandard job—invariably they must redo it. The same opportunity and obligations must be true for children. Students should not be given a bad grade and then ignored; they must be asked and guided to redo the work until they have mastered it. However, that approach would require schools to learn how to teach differently, coordinate their master schedules differently, and use out-of-the-box thinking. Our present educational system has never stopped to ask, What good is a failing grade? Whom does it benefit? If something doesn't benefit anyone, why does it exist?

The truth is, failing some students and giving others poor grades does benefit some in our society. The justifications against mastery learning are hidden below the national dialogue and are so embedded in our societal thinking that we simply don't worry about it. The educators' argument against mastery learning is that students won't work as hard if they have a "do over." That is simply nonsense and has little to no truth attached to it.

WORKING FOR SOME, FAILING OTHERS

But much more insidious is that, indeed, the present system does work for some children, not to enhance their ability to think and master skills and information, but to help their chances of advancing in society. In fact, the central core of our educational testing system has become the identification of the winners and losers. However, even the system's winners think less well, solve problems less creatively and less effectively, and are less well equipped for high-level learning than is acceptable.

In our society, parents coming from higher socioeconomic backgrounds are often aware of their ability to maintain the status quo—and they complain when the education system doesn't, to ensure that the system will benefit their own children. They exercise these prerogatives through a multitude of channels, including the act of complaining, writing to the newspapers, speaking up at public community meetings, and ultimately campaigning for the board of education themselves or convincing a friend or neighbor to run. And some even leave the public system, sending their offspring to private schools.

This more privileged group is invariably the foundation that forms and influences the local board, city council, and state legislators. As a result, these parents are the dominating voices in our society. Their children enter school with the advantage of experiential knowledge and well-connected parents—and therefore often start with a lead over other children.

These kids, too, are much more likely to have been read to, gone to the zoo, attended summer camps, traveled, and grown up in homes with parents who have time for them, and more. These children are ready for school and perform better on tests. Better test grades mean placement in advanced classes and ultimately admission to the better colleges. It is reasoned that better colleges will provide a superior education and certainly better access to contacts in society and future occupations (and professions).

Therefore, better jobs, homes, and adult lives will often follow. When it comes to our own children, we are all biased and want what is best for them. And if we don't have to consider that the system we use is hurting other people's children, so much the better.

People whose children succeed in spite of the poor practices that exist in the educational system seldom want to change the system. As much as the federal government wants to issue dire forecasts regarding the urgency of improving our educational system, policymakers do not take into account that the system also sorts, categorizes, and separates. This sorting and separation work to the advantage of some families while it unfortunately contributes to a permanent underclass.

For children who do not succeed in school, the hypocrisy is apparent, the lies are real, and the future is compromised. Kids recognize that above all else, the public schools of America are not places where they can trust their dreams to be fulfilled. Furthermore, this type of thinking places the future of the United States in jeopardy as we can no longer afford a permanent underclass and the problems associated with economic disparity.

The student who is caught in this failure chain is condemned as stupid, impaired, lazy, difficult, or worse. The greatest fear of human beings is not death—it's humiliation. Since being stupid and/or impaired is humiliating, young people consider anything better than humiliation. As a result, "lazy" and "difficult" are welcomed classifications for children who are having trouble learning. Children quickly realize that lazy and difficult people have a pattern of behavior that is also expected. Therefore, the child given these labels must act accordingly. So the very behaviors schools are trying to eradicate—e.g., tardiness, insubordination, lack of effort, absenteeism, and dropping out—are, in fact, reinforced by the American public schools.

What do children desire from the public schools? They want to trust that adults in their lives are going to make wise decisions about their education, use research to understand child development, and apply the best educational practices. And they do not want to let societal norms reinforce a status quo that condemns many of them to a substandard life. Children need adults to know that they love to learn; and when children show a lack of desire to learn or be in school, adults must consider their own practices and stop blaming the victim. What do children seek from the public schools? They want adults to recognize their own hypocritical behavior, act in ways that earn trust, and stop blaming students for problems they did not create and must live with every day at school!

BASIC CIVIL AND HUMAN RIGHTS

Children enter schools and are given the title "student." During the course of their education, children learn that the new title allows their basic human rights to be violated. They can be screamed at because their teacher is having a bad day; they can be given a punishment assignment because others were talking; they can be prevented from using a bathroom or getting a drink of water; and of course, they can often be forced to work in isolation. Arguably, for many American public school students, the concept that school is a good and desirable place quickly becomes a myth.

Even though the Supreme Court of the United States has stated in unequivocal terms that students do not check their civil rights at the schoolhouse door, in many cases, they do. As one grandparent cried to an author of this book,

> My grandson was wetting his pants at school, a practice that he had not done in a number of years. Regardless of the fact that his mother taught in the district, he was given a teacher who was creating such a hostile atmosphere, the boy was literally wetting his pants in terror. The administration of course did nothing about the teacher's approach to children and I am sure that she will continue to do this to other children for many years to come.

Children are different, as by definition they are still developing. They are not considered capable of making wise decisions regarding their own lives for many years into the future. As a result, adults are afforded great discretion regarding the treatment and nurturing of children. Unfortunately, in too many cases, in the American public schools, this "special status" has been used to take advantage of—not protect—children. Thus, the kids whom our society has afforded this "special status" to are being violated by it.

Teacher unions have become adept at protecting teachers. Of course, the unions will point out that the contractual language is designed to shield teachers from mean-spirited administrators, parents, and boards of education. In many cases, this protection is not only real, but is also fair and necessary, as teachers are often blamed for problems of schooling. Also true, the overwhelming numbers of teachers are loving and caring—and do their best for children each day. However, teachers and teachers associations, for the most part, do not consider "problem teachers" among their membership who ruin many a child's experience as their problem.

Unfortunately, as with virtually every labor association, teachers unions are notoriously bad at policing their own membership. Teachers who verbally abuse, fail to teach, and humiliate children, or otherwise violate children's rights, are protected by law, contract, and union procedures. One can only imagine the consequences for a child who wet his or her pants in school because the teacher didn't believe the kid really needed to visit the bathroom. Even more common is the story of a teacher screaming at a child to the point where others teachers stopped their teaching because of the disturbance. Predictably, the same teacher will likely repeat the same behavior each year. Every community in the United States has stories of children being verbally mistreated by adults in the public schools.

As one author (Shear) explained,

> When I took a job at an upper middle class school after teaching in a blue collar school for 12 years, I was surprised by how some of the teachers talked to students. In particular, I noticed that the same verbiage and tone that might get a teacher assaulted on hall duty in the blue collar school was common practice in the upper middle class school. I quickly realized that lower income students had enforced their own code for how they would be talked to in a hallway. The same condition did not exist in the wealthier environment as students had learned to play the game.

LIFE AT SCHOOL

Children expect the school administration and their parents to shield them from verbal abuse and other mistreatment, while they soon learn that rarely do administrators effectively protect children from this type of behavior. Kids also realize their parents and the parents association are also impotent in protecting children from the teacher whom everyone would like to avoid. What is unheard of is a state agency taking away a license from a teacher who treats children poorly. Kids know that the protection of their human rights within the schoolhouse is unlikely and that all too often, adults have a free swing at them whenever they choose. Another time, Shear explained,

> A student came in to see me on the last day of her senior year. She told me that her teacher had told a kid to f*** himself in front of the whole class and that this was a pattern of abuse towards students. She had reported it to the chairperson who had not done anything about it. When I called the chairperson down to my office, he stood in the doorway and attempted to dismiss me stating that he had taken care of it. I directed him to come into my office, sit down and tell me what he had done. It turned out he had done nothing and had given the teacher a favorable evaluation for the year and no mention of the outrageous behavior. When I held the chairperson accountable for his failure to protect the students, he told the rest of the cabinet and others how bad a person and principal I was. He never mentioned what our disagreement was about.

Administrators often fail to hold adults accountable for mistreatment of children for a variety of reasons. As a general rule, people want to be liked and school administrators are no exception. Children come and go, but staff will be there for decades. Additionally, many people are uncomfortable with situations in which they may have to confront another person. Because teachers have so much protection, disciplining them can be difficult; and as such, administrators have a built-in excuse to look the other way.

In addition, teachers are often members of the community in which they teach. They are under no obligation to tell the truth regarding an argument with the principal. In many cases, not only may they live in the community they teach in, but they may also be friends with members of the board of education. All in all, a clear picture develops as to why children often cannot expect any protection from mistreatment by school administrators.

Kids pass through the system; meanwhile, principals have to work with teachers, who are invested in the community, year after year. If a principal wants to move to another position or receive a promotion, no one checks with the students about the principal's performance. However, teachers associations are often consulted as well as ad hoc discussions held among teachers in the different districts.

All in all, no adequate procedures are set up in the American public schools to protect children from poor practices, bad treatment, and failed opportunity. Students want their basic human rights to be honored. They hope to be able to go about their day without mistreatment. They want the condition of youth to serve as a protection, not as a license to mistreat. In conclusion, what do students want? They want what adults have promised. They want adults to stop talking out of both sides of their mouth and instead play the role of protector, not victimizer.

RELATIONSHIPS, LOVE, AND FEAR

On the most literal level, human beings react to two basic emotions: love and fear. Regardless of the action or reaction of a person, it can be traced back to one of these two driving forces. Accordingly, approaches to reforming and creating better school systems are driven by one of these two basic emotions. Americans have embraced a fear-based approach to school reform. Any politician, academician, or school board member who decides it is useful to their own purposes pulls out the "fear card." They do not realize that when they use educational reform for their own advantage, and not on behalf of children, they do enormous damage to children.

Children intuitively recognize a healthy system, which evidences love, caring, joy, and meaning. Children are repelled by an unhealthy system. Children understand better than adults the effects of trying to improve school systems with the use of fear. This place of fear is perpetuated by intervention from larger outside institutions. In other words, when the federal government, giants of the business world, and other national figures make dire predictions about the future based on failing schools, they are terrifying a world that wants and needs a better life for their children.

On the school level, too often, classrooms, hallways, cafeterias, bathrooms, and school buses are places of fear. Often the conveyor of fear is a bully. Bullying can take place in many forms but often is insidious. At times the bully is an adult. Threats abound in schools. Punishment is flaunted, broadcasted, and apparent to children. Sometimes the threats take the form of denying a child the good grades necessary for admission to the college that the child is seeking; or sometimes the threat is laced with impending punishment. While consequences for poor behavior are part of the human condition, often schools use punishment in place of proactive, positive practice.

Most children adapt through compliance and use their human instincts for survival. However, adapting to the system is not easy, and it has been estimated that thirty thousand children miss school each month in the United States due to bullying and abuse. Researchers do not consider adult bullying in the equation.

Children expect adults to protect them as an outgrowth of love. That some children are victimized by screaming and threatening adults, unreasonable circumstances, and peer group bullies is an abandonment of the responsibility that adults have to their children. We know who is bullied by adults and other children—it is rarely a mystery. The abused is the child who is weaker and/or different, or who doesn't "get it," or who has been hurt by life. As a result these children are less lovable and become victims within the schoolhouse. We need to love them when they appear unlovable. As Shear explained,

> I would meet with the assistant principal of the middle school to discuss the incoming freshmen class. He told me not to worry about Joey as he would be in jail soon enough. In the first week of school I called Joey down. He had been arrested in 8th grade for assault and had a nervous tic. He wasn't overly articulate but I wasn't going to throw in the towel on him. I put together a team to support him and get him through high school. Today he is a college graduate and a member of the New York City Police Force. It wasn't rocket science; I simply cared about him when no other school official ever had. He had his ups and downs and I had to punish him from time to time, but he knew I was there for him.

Children want to be loved and they want to live in a world that is absent of fear. Abraham Maslow's hierarchy of need identified the primary importance of *safety* to human beings. Students will identify a loving environment, absent of fear, as a primary desire in what they want from schools. Unfortunately, schools are not built around the concept of love—schools rarely even consider the concept of love as a foundation principle.

Almost every adult who has gone through school has enjoyed the loving, warm environment created by at least one or two special teachers. We all understand that children want more of a feeling of love, acceptance, and belonging. Children want less of the stern educator who cares little about students as people. Children do not favor the teacher who is insistent on teaching students about responsibility. Students will learn responsibility as a byproduct of life, whether they like it or not. What students need more are role models who evidence caring, concern, and empathy.

Noblit, Rogers, and McCadden (1995) have cited "caring" as essential to education that "may guide the ways we instruct and discipline students, set policy, and organize the school day" (p. 680). Schools are not just for transmitting information or preparing one for college or the business world. Schools must teach students within a fragmented world how to care for each other. All too often, students do not see a caring figure in the front of the room. The effects of this lack of concern are at the heart of what is creating the educational outcomes that have terrified a nation. The problem is that the more worried the country gets about its schools, the more it pursues policies that stress testing and accountability. Both are enemies of caring and relationships.

CURRICULUM, PEDAGOGY, AND ASSESSMENT

The core foundation belief is that children really don't want to work and must be compelled by external rewards and punishments to learn. This concept begins with a preconceived decision that learning is "work." This notion is wrong from the outset: learning is not work—in fact, learning is a joyful endeavor that all human beings relish. What observers are witnessing and blaming on a lack of a work ethic among our students are, in fact, poor pedagogical approaches and a disconnected curriculum, which turn learning into work.

Under conditions in which instruction is boring and curriculum has little to no relation to life, learners become dissatisfied customers. In the business world, unhappy consumers are people who do not return to the business or use the product again. In most cases, these consumers do not complain; they simply do not return. The same is happening in the American schools. Each year, an overwhelming percentage of American students are rejecting their education. The Bill and Melinda Gates Foundation called this rejection of education, the *Silent Epidemic.*

The American classroom is too frequently a place in which boredom rules the day, hour by hour, minute by minute. Instructional techniques often evidence a lack of understanding of what students are experiencing and need. The present standards movement in the United States has hurt educational pedagogy on both ends of the student ability spectrum as it is bringing boredom to new levels.

High-level students, who will easily pass state assessments, are forced to sit through redundant exercises of rote memorization and the development of rather low-level skills. Remedial students are frequently given more time on task to learn the skills and curriculum that they had difficulty mastering the first time around. More times than not, the pedagogy utilized in remedial classes is repetitive and unimaginative. These are practices, then, that become nothing more than repetitive instruction. In most cases, the pedagogical framework of a "support class" hasn't changed from the original pedagogy where students didn't master the material in the first place. This repetition leaves the classroom as a place best described as a world of boredom. As Shear explained:

> I was doing a workshop with secondary principals and other supervisors of instruction. I asked them if they had sat through a double period of instruction designed for remedial learners. Not one of them had stayed for more than a single period. They freely admitted there were few things they wanted to do less than sit through a double period of remedial learning. However, the poor kids had to do it—over and over and over.

Professional development programs for pedagogical development are sorely lacking both prior to and after a teacher enters the field. The teachers—who get it and adapt their teaching to make instruction interesting and aligned with higher-order thinking skills—have for the most part taught themselves. The truth is, very few professors of education stress that being engaging, motivating, interesting, and fun is a crucial quality of excellent teaching. Students want interesting and challenging pedagogy to enjoy their day, learn, and have fun. They love learning meaningful things and no longer want to be blamed when they fail to learn meaningless things. They prefer teachers who adapt instructional techniques to meet human needs.

When it comes to the curriculum, the students want the state and the teachers to answer one critical question: Why should I learn this or that? If the state educational system, which created the curriculum, can't explain why a student should learn something, and the teacher who is charged with executing the curriculum can't understand its relevance to many students, the curriculum becomes irrelevant for everyone involved.

Frequently, business analogies are used to look at schools. If instruction were a business, when relevance was missing, the teacher would fail to make the sale. When we go into a shoe store, we don't buy an item without a reason. The same applies when we are being taught a concept. Teachers would find it incredibly helpful to link the concept being taught to a relevant factor in a student's life and society's progress. Additionally, brain research has shown that when analogies or examples that add relevance are used, the brain will store the information in multiple areas—somewhat like different file cabinets of the mind. The more areas of the brain where a piece of information is stored, the more readily the information is retrieved and utilized.

Thus, the brain can take a meaningless concept and convert it into an idea that students can relate to. For example, determining mathematically the area of a room often has little meaning to the human brain. However, when a teacher uses an example, such as asking students to determine area based on carpeting one's bedroom in bright purple carpeting, the brain stores the new information in multiple areas such as math formulas, my bedroom, purple things, and areas of the brain associated with carpeting and flooring.

A VOICE, CHANGE, AND BEAUTY

In our society, many of our schools are dilapidated structures that were built without a great deal of concern for beauty. Abraham Maslow described beauty as a human growth need. Students see their school—its condition, maintenance, and the supplies that are available for learning—as an expression of society's view of their relevance.

In many communities, the only place a child will go that is not air-conditioned is the public school. Would an adult go out to lunch on a hot day and sit in a hot restaurant? In many schools, the child does just that when entering the cafeteria of their school. What does that tell the child about the relevance of their education? Simply, children want to attend school in nice surroundings and under good conditions.

> Fifty percent of U.S. school buildings were constructed cheaply and rapidly in the 1950s and 1960s, built as if architects used cookie cutters to create classrooms, hallways, and cafeterias. Many schools need major repairs, contain environmental hazards, or exceed their planned capacity . . . architecture can facilitate cultural values, we need to look at what our present school buildings are saying to our children. (Taylor, 1993, p. 37)

Students want their classrooms, hallways, and schools to be beautiful. They want new supplies, updated textbooks, and the latest technology. They hope that their school reflects the rhetoric that society has engaged in regarding the importance of schooling. Again, in considering the structural environment and aesthetics of schools, children want the societal proclamations of importance to back up the reality of everyday life in school.

Consider this scenario: an alien from another planet peacefully lands in America. It asks to be shown around an American town, and is taken to visit the local golf course on a warm, spring day. The alien may very well remark about the beautiful lawns, the serenity of the trees, and the wonderful manner in which the land is manicured. The alien is then taken to see the local school with broken steps, classrooms in disrepair, and a general sense of malaise based on the heat students are experiencing. The alien then remarks to his earth host: "Well, your planet is different. On my planet we value our children more than our recreation."

FUN, COMMUNITY, FEELINGS, BEING IMPORTANT

One thing that students want teachers to know is that they (the children) might not recall what teachers have said, but they will always remember how teachers made them feel. More than thirty years after graduation, a woman sent this message to one of her high school teachers, as a good example of the long-term effects of caring:

> You really are too good to be true! I get more frustrated than anything. You know when I was in 2nd grade I was so dirty at school that they sent me to the showers. I thought it was cool at the time because only the older kids were able to shower at school (after gym). Anyway, I look back and it really bothers me . . . I will let you serve as my example . . . If I were half as kind as you . . . Anyway, that's probably why I liked you so much. I was the outcast and you made me feel like I wasn't.

Who is important at school? In today's schools these people are: adults, student leaders, and the athletes, as well as the really smart kids. But what if students don't have the right clothes, come from the wrong side of town, can't play sports, and struggle with school work? One would think that educational institutions would be better at handling these types of situations than any organized group.

But in many cases, children who fit into these disenfranchised categories are left to suffer alone in school. These children know they are not important; in fact, in many schools, they are considered a nuisance. In some places, children who are dirty, need extra help with their homework, and lack social skills are often viewed as lower than irrelevant. They are the type of kid that no one wants around. They are not embraced by other students, teachers, or the principal.

Of course, some teachers are saviors and some principals do fight an uphill battle for success. In fact, most teachers and principals fight on behalf of children. The problem is that too many of the bad guys in school think that they are the person who fights for social justice. Human beings are very good at self-deception, as an assistant superintendent reported:

> On a conference day, we had a guest speaker to help teachers to explore the concept of empathy. He told the story of how he was humiliated by his coach in front of the entire town. Following a bad play, the coach directed him to go into the locker room and bring back his varsity jacket and hand it in. This took place in front of a crowded gym in a small town. The teachers with empathy almost cried. The teachers without empathy, in particular one reading teacher, walked out of the presentation unmoved and convinced that she treated students well.

SUMMARY

Kids want a different experience in schools. They would like to be recognized as unhappy customers; and quite frankly, they wouldn't mind if the schools that are hurting them were closed down like a bad restaurant.

In a succinct fashion, we will list conditions that students want. We hope educational decision-makers will take note. Because if anything, America's public school students are screaming, "This place hurts my spirit" (Weeres & Poplin, 1992, p. 11).

Students want the following:

- Better Relations: Teachers treating them well, a welcoming school community, effective rules against bullying (adult and child), educational practices which introduce and reinforce how to accept people who are different from them.
- Relevance of Curriculum and Activities: If the teacher can't explain why a student needs to know information or a skill, the system is completely broken. Educators need to explore the concept of relevance in everything they teach.
- Safety: Schools must be places in which fear is a stranger!
- Importance: In the TV show *Cheers*, Norm walks into the bar and everyone yells his name. Clearly, Norm is important . . . students need to feel that in school, they are important.
- Dignity: Human dignity is at the heart of spiritual survival. Embarrassment and the compromising of any person's self-esteem are terrible things. Schools must employ practices to prevent actions that compromise a child's dignity. Differences must be celebrated not condemned. Children of different color, race, language, religion, sexual orientation, weight, height, or social class all must be accepted and touted.

- Fun and Excitement: Somehow the paradigm regarding schooling became "Learning is work." Learning is not work; it is fun and exciting. Being in a classroom should be the most exciting thing this side of Disneyland.
- Positive State and Federal Assessment Practices: Today, school districts assess learning to gather more data and to judge schools, principals, districts, and teachers, and allegedly to remediate weaker students. In truth, assessment has become another tool to force schools to be better. Not only are more evaluations not the answer, but also they hurt educational practices in numerous ways. The effects of over-evaluations are extensive—not the least of which is that high-level learners are now living in a world of rote memorization, while low-level skill practice is common practice. Thus the shrinking of both quality curriculum and the loss of exciting pedagogical practice are occurring for all students. Additionally, the testing is chronologically normed even though all do not grow up and progress at the same speed. Kids want the government to stop causing more damage.
- The End of Sorting and Separating: School testing as it progresses into the intermediate grades is designed to sort and separate the strong learners from the weak ones. The students are then separated into who will be successful and who will not. This certainly works for some, but not for the majority. Kids want to be successful, and they don't want their success stolen from them.
- To Be Treated Like a Person: This human approach includes the ability and right to drink water, go to the bathroom, move about the classroom, eat when one is hungry, hand in work late for good reasons, and more.
- Values: Students want to talk about life. They want to explore their understanding of the world. We live in a world in which the lines between what is right and wrong are so blurred that kids don't know which side they are on. If we want a better world, we

need to allot time for children to explore the concepts of right and wrong and other core values that need exploration. Maybe the adults would also learn to realign their values as well.

- The End of Hypocrisy: Kids can spot hypocrisy from a mile away. They have a more literal approach to life than adults. They see the world with a lot of the window dressing removed. Teachers want to be treated well. How many of them in turn treat children poorly simply because they can? The hypocrisy of schooling illustrates to children the wrongness of the institution of school. It reinforces for children who grow to be adults that society's promise is often absent from the public schools.

Chapter Three

Screwed-Up Educators: Finding the Path Back to Leadership

ADMINISTRATIVE-TEACHER TURF WARS

The research of Robert Marzano (2003) clearly identified the importance of a quality educator to the success of children.

> Regardless of the research basis, it is clear that effective teachers have a profound influence on student achievement and ineffective teachers do not. In fact, ineffective teachers might actually impede the learning of their students. (p. 74)

The frequent lament of teachers is that they are being held responsible for improving school outcomes without the real authority to effect change. Meanwhile, the often-heard refrain of school administrators is that they have to fix a system with employees whom they can neither fire nor even effectively discipline. Thus, teachers blame school leaders, and the leaders point to their inability to handle the shortcomings of teachers, creating this standoff at the school level indicative of a larger problem.

So, while teachers would like to blame their schools' administrators for creating an environment that disenfranchises teachers, isolating them from key decision-making, administrators meanwhile want to point the finger at teachers for politically negotiating contracts that guarantee a lack of accountability. This tension exists within schools, while the public sees educators (teachers and leaders) as one monolithic group.

Parents, students, and government are not interested in the intra-institutional finger-pointing that accompanies discussions of failing schools. The lack of teacher empowerment and of administrative discretion regarding poorly performing educators, while true, offers no comfort to non-educators. Thus, the first step for all educators—to become honestly empowered—is to realize that although they may see the teacher-administrator dynamic in terms of "us" and "them," the public is only seeing educators in terms of "them." When it comes to the lack of quality schools for their children, frustrated parents simply want to throw out the "whole bunch of them" or quit the school altogether and even leave town!

Private schools and charter schools—often boasting of a greater "spirit of cooperation"—recognize that a failure to alleviate the public school's internal dynamic of distrust would likely result in a private school going out of business, as students and their parents seek services elsewhere. Today, a growing reality is that public school teachers and administrators must come to a better understanding of the complaints of parents and students in order to survive.

This adversarial relationship between management and teachers in schools has contributed to the dynamic of government's entering into the world of school governance, regulating and overseeing both the curriculum and the assessment. Government has usurped much of what was once sacred territory for the educator. Today, the failure to come together to solve problems is one of the main reasons that Race to the Top is centered on concepts such as "teacher accountability" and the promotion of charter schools, not on educators collaborating for improvement.

Perhaps one obvious solution to the problem is a return to an old working paradigm—the concept of the "principal-teacher." The term *principal* stems from the old reality that the original school leaders were considered to be the premier or most respected "principal" *teachers*. If teaching and administrative responsibilities were better interrelated and coordinated today, perhaps it would mediate against the "us-against-them" scenario that exists in so many of America's public schools.

Thus, teachers and their principal would work together as a team to improve their schools, rather than withdrawing into their offices or classrooms and educating alone. Additionally, since the job of running a school has become so complicated and time-consuming, principals also need to share these responsibilities, for the benefit of all.

A new paradigm for schools is that administrators and teachers must come together and stop playing the "blame game" as it has contributed to the loss of their ability to lead in the effort to reform the public schools. With a collaborative new paradigm, teachers and administrators will be able to work as one—and solve problems together.

CHALLENGING THE STATUS QUO

Educators are not unique in their desire for a change from the status quo to a new collaborative "educator" approach. Few educators, were they to be asked or consulted, would disagree about the desire for a better way of collegially running schools. However, part of the human condition is to fear change, and the paralyzing effects on educators of this fear cannot be overlooked.

Educational reform, coupled with educators' instinctual fear of change, has led to a systemic paralysis and reliance on old, corporate, top-down management models. Given this paradox, when change is instituted, the system works actively to overcome and even to sabotage the new ways of operating. Even though the over-whelming percentage of educators are unhappy with the status quo, they are "more fearful" of change. When fear enters the picture, rational thinking leaves the scene.

Fear of change has left educational reform in tatters and the public strongly perceiving that educators cannot manage their own ship. In fact, the entire "standardized testing movement" is an out-growth of the belief that left on their own, educators cannot and will not solve the problems of education. When in the past educa-tors addressed the outside intervention by government to increase school accountability, teachers and administrators again did not speak with one voice. Lacking a coherent public argument from professional educators on how it should be done differently, politi-cians exploited the divisiveness for their own purposes.

Rationally, today's educational reform movement is making a very big mistake when it tries to work around educators in its effort to fix the system. Government accountability programs, such as those instituted by No Child Left Behind and Race to the Top, narrow the educational scope to a base of low-level skill assess-ments. This system, which inherently becomes a form of test prep, undercuts the great things that did occur in the American public schools. For example, the American public schools consistently produced risk takers who employed out-of-the-box thinking. How-ever, out-of-the-box thinking is likely to be one of the casualties of an accountability system based on standardized tests and prepara-tion for them.

Educators lost credibility by failing to address the low achieve-ment levels of millions of students. In particular, the poor perform-ing children were often from disadvantaged communities. Invari-ably, this failure to address the needs of low-achieving students was coupled with a built-in excuse of looking at the demographic fac-tors of the student population. While many students in these com-munities were emotionally underprepared for learning, many other children could be reached, but were not. At the same time, as educators screamed for change, they accepted the reality of the status quo.

CLEAN UP OR BE SAFE

The trickery of the human mind is at work as educators consider the concept of change. For the last thirty years, educators have considered change as both a necessity and a scary prospect, and thus have not figured out their plan for fixing the system. This cognitive dissonance, in which the human brain cannot embrace competing thoughts at the same time, has left the system stuck in between acting and fearing and thus isolated in the middle of nowhere and mediocrity. As a result, students in the American public schools have suffered.

Simply stated, this educational reform movement in which educators have systematically called for change and then feared change has led to a condition of *Screwed-up! Screwed-up* is a term we use to describe something so nonsensical that it defies logic. Kids are unhappy, educators are unhappy, parents are unhappy, and the discussion of failing schools has become a national dialogue. Still, fear of change rules the day, and educators have been reluctant to challenge misguided external interventions from government.

The choice for educators to clean up the system or be safe is a false paradigm. Preferring to be safe has actually blocked any real initiative to improve schools. As such, this lack of courage has brought to the educators who embraced the safety of the status quo a rash of undesirable change. These include the following: a dramatic upswing in home schooling, unprecedented governmental intervention on the state and federal levels, charter-school increases, inappropriate board of education interventions, new educational fads, and a rash of negative publicity.

Unfortunately, the same brain trickery that has prevented educators from employing successful interventions is still at work. Make no mistake about it: the interventions by Race to the Top will face tremendous resistance from a collective culture that is well versed in stopping change. However, the same minds that are stopping change are not only hurting children but also self-destructing. Slowly and in an evolutionary way, educators are losing control of the public schools because leaders will not recognize, address, and cure the disease.

Educators can gain the empowerment necessary to fix the system so they can once again be masters of their own house. However, this process is going to require collective leadership on the administrative and teacher fronts to embrace change, based on market research about their consumer. This idea has not been embraced and is rarely discussed in the world of educational reform. Cleaning up the system requires stopping and reversing the screwed-up continuum.

The only way that educators are going to feel comfortable within their own environment is if they gain control of the educational world in which they reside. Unfortunately for educators, the government's encroaching and the media's second-guessing are unlikely to go away. The only way educators are going to regain control of the American public schools is to improve the system in its own right. Safe is no longer a long-term option in the world of public education. As long as the public is angry about the fate of their children in the public schools, the outside "assault" will continue.

Educators must come together and speak with one voice, as they need to tell the public what they will do to fix the broken school system. They should show research and evidence that their ideas are better than the outside interventions offered by the government.

As a new paradigm, educators should embrace change and not be afraid of new methods for operating schools. The failure on the part of educators to meet the new challenge, using a new paradigm, is destroying the public schools as we know them. And this failure is leaving an arguably worse model in their place.

THE ARGUMENT FOR EDUCATIONAL EMPOWERMENT

Intuitively, it is crazy to empower a group that has failed to fix a problem for decades. Common sense would dictate that outside intervention is necessary to remedy the plight of the American public school student. But as we have indicated, trusting the brain is a slippery slope. Educators are the single best solution for saving our public schools. We have already seen that outside interventions are frequently as misguided as they are well intended. Enlightened educators are uniquely located to fix the system.

Human nature tends to overcorrect when problems arise. Rather than making a small change that will have a major impact, we tend to overcorrect and cause problems in an equal and opposite direction. Hence, now that the government has got involved with the standardized test format for school accountability, in effect, government officials are succeeding in sucking the system dry of creativity, fun, and out-of-the-box thinking—first paralyzing educators and subsequently affecting students.

The overcorrection to help students with low academic skills has constrained the education of students on the other end of the spectrum. Mid-level and high-performing students are repeatedly prepped to do well on low-level, meaningless assessments. And American public schools see less creative thinking as a result.

Some educators know better than to strip the educational landscape of creativity, imagination, exploration, and discovery while politicians and state and federal educational bureaucrats simply do not understand the consequences of their actions. Too many schools in America are restricting free time, narrowing curriculum, and curtailing festivals and celebrations in the name of "doing better on the next test." The governmental and educational bureaucrats, though they have good intentions, have brought a "pox" into the American public schools—all in the name of accountability and improvement. Many educators simply know better.

The adjustment that educators need to make includes changing their baseline paradigms about schooling. Once this is accomplished (although it will take considerable effort to defeat the brain that will fight for the status quo), the educators have the potential to set up a school system that will be the envy of the world. Educators must embrace this approach; for while they are wonderful interventionists, they have been terrible diagnosticians.

Educators have seen the world of education as one in which students do not cooperate and must be coerced to learn. They have created strong interventions—so strong that students have run away from the system. The problem, of course, is that the interventions have been gauged to cure the wrong disease.

The byproducts of running schools in violation of the basic rights of children are what educators have been observing—and not an inherent laziness on the part of children. Again, educators have been very weak at diagnosing what causes the problems that they are observing. Once educators understand that they have been giving the wrong medicine because they have diagnosed the wrong disease, school improvement will accelerate at an unprecedented rate.

Despite popular belief, educators get it. They do not deny that the school systems are failing children. However, they have felt overwhelmed in their individual ability to effect change. They have been going in the wrong direction and have gotten lost in a forest of reform, outside intervention, fear, and misdirection. Once educators understand where they went awry, the schools of America will quickly go from screwed-up to stepping-up on behalf of the kids.

The vast majority of educators love children and want to do their best on behalf of those whom they are empowered to protect. They just need the right medicine to cure the patient.

PROFESSIONAL *UNDERDEVELOPMENT*

Perhaps the most useless enterprise in education has been "professional development." Educators have been offered a series of academicians, consultants, retirees, and local initiatives, all in the name of making them better educators. Although professional development is mandated in many states, teachers and administrators will point to very few instances in which the classroom practices of a teacher have been greatly changed or enhanced by these efforts.

Once again, we need to revisit why something went wrong in education, starting with educating the educators. Their professional development is built on a foundation consisting of traditional practices, new trends, identified needs, and alleged best practices. If each of these four is based on an incorrect paradigm, educators are going to be spinning their wheels as they implement interventions that result in little to no improvement.

Once a veteran teacher has seen enough interventions that have made no discernible difference, a perpetual sense of cynicism takes hold. This doubt is followed by frustration, anger, and a sense that things will never really get better. And teachers continue with a lack of skill development that would make their jobs and days more rewarding. As one teacher explains,

> I go home some nights and I cry until I feel really foolish. I'll have one day that will go good and I will be so excited with my students. Then I'll turn around on any other day and do any of the same kinds of activities and they will just be devastating. The attitude will be here as they come in the door. I've remained very calm because that's my nature. I am not the kind of teacher

up to this point who easily sends students out of my room because it's my feeling always that when they're not in my room they can't learn.

I need them in here. I think that maybe I let that go too far only because I kept thinking I could make a difference. Maybe there are some students that I can't make a difference with and that hurts, just having to say that hurts a lot. But, there's an anger. Sometimes, I don't know where it's coming from. I don't think it's coming from in here. But there is an anger that I don't know how to deal with. [Silence.] I don't know how to deal with it (middle school teacher). (Weeres & Poplin, 1992, pp. 12)

Imagine a scenario in which a person needs to call a plumber to stop a leak under his/her kitchen sink. The water is going everywhere, and the plumber comes in without his tools. He has no wrench to tighten the pipes, no replacement parts, and simply has his hands. So he goes over to the pipe that is leaking and tries to tighten the connection with his bare hands. Obviously he fails and he gets soaked in the process. He is angry, the owner is stressed, and the water continues to go everywhere. This chaos is exactly the situation that our public school teachers face every day.

Teachers' tools are skills and a knowledge-base on handling situations, children, curriculum, pedagogy, and more. They simply are going into classrooms day after day without the necessary tools. Unlike the plumber, they were neither given a toolbox nor the right tools. Their toolbox is filled with professional development that has failed to work on the undergraduate, graduate, and professional levels. We simply have an epidemic in the classroom of willing hands lacking the appropriate tools.

It is easiest to go through an open door. But what happens if the door is not only not open, but also doesn't really exist in the first place? Then the only solution is to grab a hammer, a saw, some wood, and nails—and to build a door. Teachers and administrators have traditionally awaited excellent professional development help from the outside. Universities were expected to train teachers, and then their professors would form a cottage industry of doing professional development activities for teachers already on staff. The problem is that the university training and the professional development initiatives have frequently fallen short of what is needed.

Public school educators have to go back to the drawing board and build their own door. Teachers unions, districts, and other internal sources should be tapped to identify the best and brightest innovations that have had the most outstanding results. Their brilliance must be used in professional development efforts. With today's ability to use blogs, websites, and other methods for communication, the messages from the best and brightest can be spread easily and efficiently. In fact, public schools and teachers associations can compete to set up the best website for professional development and be rewarded with monetary awards for making quality information available.

Also, an overabundance of educational research is available in today's world of professional development. The problem is that an efficient sorting of the research has not been used to highlight the important "best practices." For example, frequently in this book we include information from a 1991 study conducted by the Institute for Education in Transformation at the Claremont Graduate School (Weeres & Poplin, 1992). The study reinforced the opinion of psychiatrist Dr. William Glasser that in education, we are attempting to cure the symptoms and not the disease. The report cited seven issues that are at the heart of the problems of America's public schools. But as often happens, many important pieces of educational research were lost among the morass of information regarding education.

FRUSTRATIONS

The hallways and classrooms of America's public schools are filled with a cadre of professional educators drowning in a sea of frustration. Educators' lives feature a host of newfound responsibilities with less authority to control their classrooms and schools than ever before. Schools, once the domain of the local community, have been invaded in the last four decades by state and federal policies and interventions. The state and federal governments have encroached on curriculum and assessment to the point that educators are often unable to correct decisions that are hurtful to children.

For example, the New York math curriculum is a living case of the failure to protect children from the state. In the mid-1990s, the state changed the curriculum to feature two high-school-level courses that would each run for a year and a half. Principals and teachers warned the state that this "carry-over" of curriculum between school years was not in the best interests of the students.

Furthermore, the state employed floating cut points for a passing grade, meaning that the number of correct answers necessary to achieve an A—or even a passing grade—would be different from year to year.

This double folly led to a catastrophe: a number of years into the plan, over 70 percent of the students who sat for the exam failed. The state finally admitted that their curriculum—which was presented over a year and a half—and their method for achieving the passing score were flawed. They announced that they would fix what they had broken. Unfortunately for teachers and administrators, who are trying to protect children, the change would take five additional years to implement.

The world of the educator is filled with first-hand knowledge of the loss of student potential and lives that await adults who are not successfully re-corrected. Surprisingly, many of the educators who burn out first are the ones who are most passionate about children.

Teachers find it is extraordinarily difficult to care about children, want to make a difference, and be beaten down each day by a bureaucracy that seems to stall change at every turn. Again a teacher explains,

> It's not a job for me. Um, this is embarrassing; it's a calling. I think people are called to teach. I don't mean that in a religious sense. But I am truly happiest when immersed in these problems with students, but it's been very tiring and I would like to feel positive more than I do now. (middle school teacher; Weeres & Poplin, 1992, p. 32)

The public educational system overwhelms educators with society's problems, demanding a quick fix in schools that all too often lack the appropriate resources. When studying the frustration of schooling, we can start with the overwhelmed, under-supported American school principal. Virtually all studies on education look to the principalship as a key factor in successful schools. Yet these administrators are less empowered than ever before with demands from government, boards of education, superintendents, and teachers unions—leaving principals behind schedule virtually all the time. Seemingly, they have to do their real job of being an educational leader in their spare time, as one principal explains,

> All at the same time I had a teacher on the intercom—emergency. My office was full of kids. Child Protective Services shows up and is on a time constraint. Police officers come in to see a student I had called about. Parents come to pick up a student just suspended and they are not happy and this is all going on at the same time. You never go home saying I fixed that. You know it's never fixed. It's like your kitchen floor. You mop it. Darn it, somebody is gonna walk on it again and there you're gonna be. (principal; Weeres & Poplin, 1992, p. 33)

Thus, one of the constraints on empowering educators is time. We have asked them to do more things with fewer hours. This problem is only getting worse with a lack of funds in society to support education. We want everything from our educational leaders and teachers, but the reality of their day can be hellish. Today's teachers frequent faculty rooms less often, enjoy each other's company less often, and communicate less often than their colleagues of a few decades ago.

A "perfect storm" of situations has contributed to the mess. Test prep practices, growing societal problems, shrinking levels of support, and increased demands from our special education population—including a much higher percentage of children on the autistic spectrum—have made time to "think" a rare event.

We cannot empower or expect our educators to solve the problems of schools when we ignore the time constraints plaguing the field. Frustration, anger, and sometimes rage occur when educators see what has happened to the world of education. Their voice needs to be part of the solution, but it cannot be if they do not even have time to go to the bathroom during the school day. Perhaps, the first act of empowerment may be to explore better uses of time and how to help support educators as they attempt to find their way out of the morass of jobs to which they are now assigned.

ADDRESSING THE COMPLAINTS

Be it an educational institution or business, a great road map to improvement seeks the integration of consumer complaints into the reform program. Educators have blamed the student, parent, society, a lack of resources, poor working conditions, each other, and a myriad of other factors for the undesirable educational outcomes we live with.

The customers don't care who's to blame, as they simply want the problem solved, immediately, or they want a choice to go somewhere else. The paradigm that the system is what it is and is unchangeable is casting a death sentence on public education. Educators seem to be missing that the political urgency for "school choice" is the equivalent of consumers declaring that they will never go back to that restaurant.

Educators will gain empowerment when they finally recognize they must change based on qualitative and quantitative market research. As qualitative market research often can be found in unsolicited comments, feedback surrounds the field. For example, a few decades ago, American song writer Paul Simon wrote in "Kodachrome," "When I think back on all the crap I learned in high school, it's a wonder I can think at all." This statement could serve as the educational anthem of a generation.

Educators and schools of education must emphasize "relationship-based training." The most frequent complaint of parents and students is regarding treatment. Parents want teachers who will love their children. Parents need educators who will communicate with them so a team approach can be instituted for the good of the child. A parent whose child usually brings home a grade of 95 doesn't want their first notification of their child's marking-period grade as an 82 on a report card: they want a phone call while they can still effect change.

A failure to address complaints is the major reason that educators have lost so much control of the key decisions in public schools. Teachers are organized into associations that have largely decided that their role in the public schools is to defend people within their organization who are under threat from administration. It does not matter whether the administration is right; the teacher still receives a strong defense. As a result, a permanent underclass of inferior teachers has been protected, and it has thrived. However, no action comes without a cost, and this position has come at the expense of assumed teacher competence for the great majority of dedicated educators.

TEACHERS ASSOCIATIONS AND A NEW PARADIGM

Teachers associations became empowered since, when allowed, school districts simply did not negotiate in good faith. Teachers were not only poorly paid, but they were also taken advantage of in multiple ways. In the late 1960s Albert Shanker and the New York City United Federation of Teachers went on strike over poor pay and other labor-related issues. Realizing the power-block that teachers had created, politicians supported legislation that balanced labor negotiations. As a result, pay, benefits, and professional obligations swung toward teachers. In fact, in many cases, the balance swung too far toward teachers.

In many public schools, we have teachers who believe they can create their own professional obligations. In fact, they are right as contracts have allowed teachers to take liberties that are not always in the best interest of kids or, in the long run, the teachers. Parent contact, extra help, and a myriad of other obligations are too often at the discretion of the teacher. Arguably, nothing has fueled parents' frustration more than the non-responsive educator who is not doing right by their children. As a result, charter schools have flourished and continue to gain momentum.

Probably the single biggest difference between a public school and a charter school is teacher attitude. For the most part, charter-school teachers are hired with a clearer understanding of the expectation to provide service to children and parents than their counterparts in the traditional public school. However, many charter schools have also floundered as a result of poor practices.

In the twenty-first century, teachers associations will recognize the role that attitude has played in the problems associated with the public schools. While the public school teacher did not create the problems that students bring to the schoolhouse—and at times the problems appear overwhelming—the teacher must find new resources to solve problems and communicate with parents. Teachers associations are risking their existence and the future of American public schools by allowing teachers with bad attitudes to survive and thrive in the system. The time for educators to clean up the bad eggs in their profession is now.

While teachers associations still command a great deal of clout in state capitals, an unstoppable demand for tenure reform is rising, and state after state will consider issues regarding teacher tenure. The day of an incompetent teacher's surviving and thriving is being challenged across the country. Shear explained how these situations usually unfold:

> I came in as the new principal and I looked at the passing and mastery rate for the New York State Regents in the different courses. I had one teacher who had only two students in seven years get over a 90 on the state exam. I called in the chairperson who was new to the job but not the district. She acknowledged that he was incompetent. In fact, a student who went out ill fired him as her home tutor because the student claimed she knew more than he did. Four years and many negative evaluations later, the district still did not want to take on a tenure hearing because the chances of winning it were very poor.

The new paradigm going forward is that teachers groups must become professional organizations that self-regulate. Additionally, professional standards must be enforced by teachers themselves if they want to be major players in the next era of school reform. It is simply time for teachers associations to reflect honestly on the role that they have not played and start playing it.

THE LEAP TO BEING A PROFESSION

Teachers are very quick to inform anyone who asks that they are a member of a true profession, like medical doctors and lawyers. However, professions are self-regulating: doctors are regulated and reviewed by the American Medical Association; lawyers are reviewed by the American Bar Association. Teachers would like to consider themselves as professionals, and they describe themselves as professionals. But they do not meet the strict definition of a profession. Dan Lortie in his classic book *Schoolteacher* (1975) calls teachers "semi-professionals" for this reason.

For the most part, teachers are resigned to allowing administrators to perform the review of their performance and to allow the legal apparatus of the states to deal with license review and extreme issues. Teachers do not want to sit in judgment of their colleagues for three reasons: (1) it is uncharted territory that makes them uncomfortable; (2) license review is a distasteful job best left to others; and last but not least, (3) the present apparatus for teacher review, even in cases of gross misbehavior, is substandard. In most cases, problem teachers simply walk away with minimal consequences.

But other professionals help their colleagues, guide them, evaluate them, and promote them, whether it's professors in universities, doctors in practice, or lawyers in their law firms. Thus, teachers have long struggled to attain professional status (see Lortie, 1975; Etzioni, 1969), while also pursing union organization to improve their pay and benefits.

SUMMARY

The world of educators is a complicated morass of caring, loving individuals who are desirous of change and yet fearful of it. The reform movement of the last several decades is based on an unspoken assessment by the public that left to their own devices, educators will not fix America's public schools.

The truth is, America has demanded more of its public schools than one could reasonably expect. The reality of America is a world in which the middle class is shrinking, language-challenged immigrants abound, and greater numbers of disabled children are entering the system. Although American educators are unfairly judged and held responsible for things that are out of their control, the reality remains that they still haven't done their best in improving the areas of schooling within their control.

Educational decision-makers have allowed poor administrators, teachers, and superintendents to survive and thrive. They have not taken a strong enough stand on self-regulation and evaluation, on professional development, and on meeting the needs of parents and children. Most importantly, they have allowed much of the decision-making about how to educate children to be stripped away by government.

Educators, operating with the foundation principle of meeting the expressed needs of children and parents, are the best answer to the dilemma of fixing the American public schools. Our perpetual reform movement is a definitive indication that schools are in trouble and solutions have not worked. A reengaged, professional class of educators with appropriate professional development is our best bet to end the constant search for new solutions.

However, for educators to reclaim stewardship over the public schools, they must embrace the principles of consumerism. Students and parents need to have their feedback serve as a road map for educators to initiate a series of changes designed to create satisfied consumers. For educators, it is the only true course back to empowerment. Additionally, educator-led reform based on consumer satisfaction is the best formula for getting it right for the next generation of American students.

Chapter Four

Screwed-Up by Government and Governance

GOVERNMENT AND THE MISGUIDED EFFORT

The problems with governmental interventions in schools are two-fold. First, the government, like every other portion of American society, has the wrong foundation paradigms about schooling. Once again, the core problem of the American public schools is that for an overwhelming percentage of students, schools are places in which joy and emotional fulfillment are nearly absent.

Government actions to alleviate the problem of dropouts and poor test performance have not identified the absence of student happiness and satisfaction as the problem permeating the system. The concept of treating children with love as a main ingredient for academic success has never been discussed in state capitals or Washington, DC, much less our local school districts.

The second problem is that government has proven itself repeatedly incapable of learning from prior mistakes in its attempt to improve the American public schools. Because of the power of government, the mistakes have been very damaging—and thus severely threatening to the things American schools do well. For example, Americans have traditionally been risk-takers and entrepreneurs who think out of the box.

Today's education system has reverted to the goal of having kids succeed on low-level state assessments, instead of seeking to fulfill the real potential of all students. Certainly, the best and the brightest among our children deserve a better education than one consumed with obtaining success on low-level assessments. And the average and less able students should have exciting and creative ways to learn and improve.

When considering the public schools, government officials have had a difficult time finding genuine answers as the public continues to demand better schools. Politicians have continually fallen into the "Screwed-Up" mold as they have attempted external "fixes" for a system that eludes easy analysis. Elected officials think that they have been working to solve the problems of public schools—while, in reality, they have really been trying mainly to please their constituents. Some might argue that catering to constituents who are parents will help the schools. But political "quick fixes" to gain voter approval are often misguided and ineffective in improving schools.

The public schools have long been the domain of local communities, a concept that has eroded over the latter part of the twentieth century; and thus the problems of the public schools have found their way to Washington. Three out of the last four presidents have attempted to "fix the public schools" with major interventions.

In 1989, President George H. W. Bush unveiled Goals 2000, attempting to establish national purposes for education. Under President George W. Bush, No Child Left Behind continued Washington's intervention by creating minimum accountability standards for schools. Similarly for the third leader, President Obama's Race to the Top has continued Washington's intervention with bucket loads of money, spent in uneven ways, focusing on changing teacher and principal accountability ratings. But Race to the Top has not sufficiently considered why the two prior reform movements have not changed the educational landscape.

All three have been based on incorrect paradigms. While it's true that schools should have significant goals—and teachers, principals, and schools should be held accountable—these are not the key reasons schools fail. Rather, these three programs (Goals 2000, No Child Left Behind, and Race to the Top) are part of a system that has consistently refused to incorporate the views of parents, students, and educators in assessing education. As such, this matrix must include in its formulation a rating system that reflects parent and student experiences and satisfaction with the educational experience.

A NEW PARADIGM FOR GOVERNMENT AND THE PUBLIC SCHOOLS

The Politicians' Great Deception

Schools need honest partners in their efforts to help children. Unfortunately, government officials have been much more comfortable using schools as scapegoats and/or as political issues to throw out in their campaign for their own betterment. Instead, government officials first have to decide in working with schools: Are they politicians or statesmen? Politicians will sustain, perpetuate, and even worsen the problem. Statesmen will stop misleading people about schools, and move to engage educators and families in the process of reform.

The fact is, schools are a mirror of society, and they reflect the community and the student body from which they are derived. High-wealth, high-achieving parental communities will often have children who perform well on standardized tests, supporting their offspring and the schools that they attend (e.g., through higher local property tax contributions, more involvement and attendance at school board and school site meetings, and a more focused response to problems in their children's schools).

In fact, the correlation between local wealth and SAT outcomes is real and substantial. However, too many communities have children who are raised in a variety of poor, unhealthy environments (see Cooper & Mulvey, 2012). What politicians will not admit and statesmen must is that the schools are not broken, the greater society is. For example: A New York City assistant principal reported to Shear, the following story:

> I was an assistant principal in a New York City middle school and was called to a class because the students were staring at a dead body outside the window on the sidewalk. Because of room shortages, she had no other location to move the students to. She sought out the principal who directed her to close the blinds on the window. The assistant principal informed the principal that the windows hadn't had blinds for the last few years.

Another example: New York State composed a rating system for schools labeled "similar schools." The basis for placement in a "similar school category" was community wealth and student poverty. Thus, schools with high poverty rates were not expected to perform as well on standardized assessments when compared with "wealthier schools." Less was expected of these poorer schools and for good reason: these schools were populated by a disproportionate number of at-risk kids. "Categorization" was a way of "writing off" the poorer schools, rather than taking each school as a unique institution with its own strengths, resources, and skills.

The extraordinary thing about "similar schools" is that it was not *considered* extraordinary but rather was deemed necessary, practical, and reality based. In other words, from day one of the accountability system, the state was admitting that some schools can be expected to have lower outcomes than other schools because of poverty, and the state actively categorized them that way. Poor was poor, and rich was rich. However, as state mandates for improved performance have been issued, no secret formula has descended from Washington or state capitals on how best to improve outcomes for kids from ravaged neighborhoods.

In Helping the Public Schools, Government Must Get Better, a Lot better!!!

The government at all levels can be a powerful agent of positive change. Given government's perpetual failure in the school reform movement, we are tempted to call for the removal of federal and state governments from the process of schooling, leaving the system to local communities, parents, and political leaders. National and state interventions have been at best ineffective and, at worst, incredibly damaging.

But, the power of government to be a force for good is much too important to be dismissed. Government is needed to end the Screwed-Up condition in which the public schools have operated, often not in the best interest of children. Government is the single entity most capable of enacting widespread change in the shortest period of time. The key for governments on the state and national level is to get on the right road for school improvement, and soon. A continued failure of government to consider students and educators in the dialogue of reform is one of its biggest mistakes.

Government can enact appropriate reform; but first it has to figure out what "appropriate reform" is. This section maps out the relationships that governmental leaders should establish with educators and the steps they should take in making school improvement. These government actions should include making schools safe and helping those students who are most at-risk of failure, while also improving conditions for our top learners.

GOVERNMENT AND SAFETY

Maslow's hierarchy articulated the importance of *safety* in human decision-making. A sense of safety and well-being is crucial to a healthy life and the ability to focus on growth and improvement. The reality of safety is probably the greatest area of disconnect between the stated intentions of government and the reality of governance. Government has continually played a blame game with schools for all of the societal issues that reach the schoolhouse door. In New York State, for example, schools have to file an annual discipline report with the state revealing the incidents that have occurred in buildings, although the state has taken no real action to make the schools safer.

Government has failed miserably to create safe neighborhoods for our children. Furthermore, government has been unable or unwilling to make laws that allow for school administrators to deal effectively with dangerous students. Authorities completely shirk their responsibility in this area as they blame the last one on the food chain—the school official—for the situation and subsequent safety problem.

If state legislators had to fear going to the bathroom when they were in a legislative session, or if they were at risk of being beat up by a gang member if they bumped into the wrong legislator in the hallway, laws would be made to protect the lawmakers. In schools across America, known predators walk freely through the hallways because the legislatures and courts have guaranteed their rights.

Unfortunately, the right of the everyday student to rely on school safety in an environment conducive to learning has *not* been protected in the same way. There is no need to; politicians have someone else to blame for the problem in school administrators. Principals are left on their own to establish relationships and figure out ways to deal with potentially violent situations. As Shear explained:

One of our African-American students had just been released from the County Jail in time to start classes in September. An Hispanic street gang tried to move in on his business during the summer. The student ran down the street after a car-load of drug dealers shooting his gun. When the police arrived, the gun had been thrown away and no one would testify against the student. He was still taken into custody and held for several weeks.

Upon release, he came to the opening day of school and the assistant principal and I were waiting for him. He saw us as two white men—but white men who cared about him and wanted him to have a good life. We reminded him he could not bring a gun to school. He laughed and told us he would never do that. We were curious and asked him why he would never bring a gun to school. He said, he didn't want to be suspended (apparently our relationship meant a great deal to him) and then he said, I don't need a gun in school—who is going to f*** with me?

When it comes to safety for our kids in school, we need politicians to become statesmen. We require laws and programs designed to protect the innocent. We need the rule of law to stop the "Screwed-Up" situation in which predators have "rights" and innocent children are substantially unprotected. We should insist on a new paradigm from state legislators to think out of the box to protect children. These new paradigms may include the following considerations:

- *The creation of special counseling schools for dangerous students.* The courts have maintained that every child is deserving of an education, and outplacement is very expensive. If the state took this responsibility from local schools and communities, schools would become immediately safer. These schools could then work on skills, counseling, and increasing student graduation rates. It is crucial that society create therapeutic-school placements for our most dangerous students. Absent appropriate intervention, these children will hurt people and spend a life in and out of prison. The expense of prison is so exorbitant that in addition to it being a moral imperative to help these kids, it is also economically prudent. In a society that seldom thinks about the long-term expense of a failure proactively, this would be a great societal improvement.

- *A panel for reviewing the actions of inappropriate parents, coupled with laws holding parents accountable for being inadequate parents.* Society has allowed a condition in which inappropriate parents are relieved of their personal responsibility for their own child. We are advocating laws holding parents accountable in family court for a failure to live up to "societal expectations" in raising their children, especially when parents encourage their children toward violence.

- *Special laws protecting school officials such as those that exist for police officers.* School administrators, particularly those in charge of discipline and student (mis)behavior, should be protected as a police officer is with a higher criminal classification for those who assault them.

- *Abolition of a child and parent's right to interview a witness against their child if the witness is another student regarding an assault or violent action.* Instead of a victim having to face the person who hurt him or her in a hearing, we should allow an independent official appointed by the state to pose questions to the child without exposing the child's identity. It is a more reasonable solution to provide the principal with wider discretion for making judgments regarding matters involving student witnesses. Government must balance the rights of the accused in a school hearing with the rights of the victim. Today, the law mandates that schools operate as if they were courts of law. Therefore, the rights of the victim are minimal in comparison to the rights of the accused. This does not work when attempting to create safe schools.

GOVERNMENT AND ACCOUNTABILITY

In today's reform movement, government officials consider the answer for educational reform to be holding teachers and principals accountable for student performance on standardized assessments.

As a result, Race to the Top is mandating new accountability measures for teachers and principals. The process is being augmented by the stress of Washington's withholding funding from states unless they comply with new professional assessment procedures. As a result, states are putting into effect accountability systems that Washington views as favorable.

As always, student and family inputs are absent from the accountability system. Additionally, students' problems and perceived needs are not part of the dialogue. As far as the federal Department of Education is concerned, students only need to do better on an annual assessment that means nothing to them or their future.

In many states, for example, the move is to use a numerical rating system that will place principals and teachers in acceptable or unacceptable categories. Under Freedom of Information laws (FOIL), numeric indicators are "FOILable." In other words, the evaluation score of each individual teacher is likely to wind up in the local newspapers. Bureaucrats rarely think of the consequences of their actions.

Under this system, many teachers will be more concerned with their individual score as determined by students' improvement on a standardized assessment than the emotional growth and well-being of their students. Will Washington officials get it when their children come home night after night with five to ten hours of homework assigned by an anxious core of teachers interested in their own rating, and thus their survival?

Perhaps many public officials will not see the consequences of their actions in their own homes, as their children may attend private schools. These institutions have been left alone by the political flurry which has inflicted upon the public schools the wrong medicine to cure the disease.

The amazing thing about the accountability movement (which features a numerical teacher rating) is not that it's being implemented. Rather, it is that some public officials actually think it will work. These officials believe that if they hold people's feet to the fire, these expectations will improve students' performance on standardized tests.

Again, an accountability measure is only worth as much as the assessment and the ability of teachers to understand what is being tested and the results. Additionally, the greater understandings of life—the items that would be considered "higher-order thinking skills"—are for the most part absent from standardized assessments.

Government officials are foolish to think that a numerical accountability system will do more than the traditional summative written narratives of performance that are standard in the education industry. For the same reasons, summative evaluations are "soft," and numerical ones can also be expected to fall short of desired outcomes. The developers of this new accountability measure are missing the point that people are easily able to circumvent evaluation systems.

For an example, take a look at the evaluative system that Congress has used to avoid accountability. Districts are gerrymandered to provide politicians with favorable districts in which to run for office. Fund raising rules are allowed to be incredibly loose because incumbents are the ones who receive the funds. Sitting legislators are given discretionary funds to give out as gifts in the community as they see fit—money that comes with strings attached. And interest groups strongly fund an incumbent who is on their side.

All in all, unless a severe economic downturn or another exceptional problem occurs, incumbents are reelected to Congress well into the 90th percentile. Therefore, politicians have found a way around the accountability process of direct elections. Do they think the people who taught them will not be able to come up with a process to circumvent their new accountability system as well?

Another hypocrisy of the new New York State system that assigns an actual score to principals' and teachers' names is that school district superintendents are not held equally accountable. Chief executive officers of a school district are not to be evaluated using the same system, nor will they be subject to the evaluation process; but they will be able to use the scores against their principals and teachers.

In places in which superintendents change frequently, the best defense a principal will have against a new hostile superintendent is good public relations. Much of reputation in small communities comes from what the school faculty says within a community about their principal. If principals want good public relations stemming from the faculty, the principals will be sure that the faculty gets good numeric reviews.

This numeric accountability system is thus another example of governmental interference with schools without considering the negative side effects. It is bureaucracy run mad, a fear-based system meant to appease the press and public. The system of accountability reflects a legitimate frustration with educators who are in the system and who do not pull their own weight. However, numeric ratings are not an answer, and they will make things worse for children, not better!

GOVERNMENT AND BOARDS OF EDUCATION

Simply stated, the government wants it both ways in dealing with local boards of education. As federal and state governments are in an unprecedented wave of intervening in local affairs through the implementation of accountability standards, school boards are completely left alone. The government wants to establish and guarantee that the local boards have a mandate over actions within their school districts. Yet at the same time, authorities are ignoring that the school board and the chief executive officer of a school district have ultimate responsibility for what transpires in the district.

Furthermore, mandates for the training of and job requirements for school boards are for the most part absent from the equation. As a result, local school boards are often on one pole or the other of internal school governance. As a result of not knowing what they are and are not supposed to do, many school boards are intervening in areas in which they do not belong. On the other end of the spectrum are the school boards that do not supervise the district to any reasonable level. Both types of school board are unacceptable, as one fails to provide substantive oversight, while the other type of board creates an inappropriate control and management dimension.

Of course, some school boards are effective and act appropriately. The problem is that government has done little to nothing to affect the conditions that create appropriate local governance and to recognize the outcomes for children. Government has taken a "benign neglect" approach to boards of education and conveniently ignores blatant problems. As such, government is letting children and schools down. Governmental oversight must intervene to create effective mandates for the operation and review of school boards, using results to help schools improve.

One of the biggest issues in schools, and one that needs to be a greater part of the everyday discussion, is how school boards have approached their fiduciary responsibilities to oversee public funds.

Now after the Roslyn, New York, school scandal in which the superintendent and assistant superintendent engineered the theft of millions of district dollars, we see a need for more transparency.

Following the scandal, New York State began requiring training for school board members. It is long overdue for government to have created a public spending matrix to compare where and how districts expend their money. Determining how much money, for example, goes to teachers, administrators, materials, testing, etc., will be a very effective place to begin comparing equity in education and improving spending for all children.

PROFESSIONAL CONTRACTS THAT WORK FOR KIDS

One of the functions at which school boards have frequently proved themselves most inept is contract negotiations with unions of teachers and other employees. Virtually all employee units and the superintendents have negotiated contracts over the last few decades that screw-up kids in one way or another. The fact of the matter is that kids are not a major part of the dynamic of contract negotiations. This type of oversight is a concept that will be disputed by many educators; however, in contract negotiations, individuals and units negotiate on behalf of their own self-interests.

Contracts contain items that make changing an educational practice more difficult than knocking down the brick walls that constitute the school. Although each district's contract differs, it is not unusual to find teacher contracts that restrict the time of each period, the starting and closing time of the school day, limits on the ability of the administration to observe classroom practices at free will, minimal requirements for teachers to provide extra help to students, and very few other professional requirements for treatment and care of students. Additionally, the observed treatment of pupils is rarely incorporated into the document used to formulate teachers' end-of-the-year evaluations.

Superintendents' contracts have become extremely lucrative in certain parts of the country over the last two decades. While few would argue about the difficulty and importance of the top district post, the percentage salary, benefits, and increases above those of principals and teachers over the last quarter century point out an advantage in pay and benefits for superintendents who negotiate their own contract with a board of education. Additionally, the contracts are usually one-sided in that superintendents routinely break the contract if a better offer comes their way, while boards are forced to maintain their end of their bargain if they have agreed to a multi-year contract.

All of this occurs as the governing agencies in state capitals and Washington, DC, sit on the sidelines. The states can easily make restrictions as to what can and cannot go into a collective bargaining agreement of a public school, as well as what can and cannot be written into a contract between a board of education and a superintendent. Again, government conveniently sits out the fight when kids need better policies the most, while at the same time, government gets involved in things that are just foolish in comparison.

GOVERNMENT AND TENURE

Tenure was created to allow teachers to explore controversial concepts without fear of retribution or firing, not to protect teachers who are substandard, mean spirited, or mentally ill. The vast majority of teachers meet standards, are not mean spirited, and are mentally healthy. What does permeate the field is a lack of professionalism regarding the obligations that accompany the field of teaching.

Communications with parents is one of the least desired aspects of a teacher's professional duties, as these parent-teacher contacts can be time-consuming, and many parents can be inappropriate and difficult over issues regarding their children. However, this relationship is a professional obligation and an important one.

Professional responsibilities extend to working reasonably in response to district and administrative directives. Many teachers are resistant to the educational fads that permeate the field. Additionally, teachers are frequently suspicious of administrators and their ability to supervise instruction. However, professionalism requires a reasonable level of cooperation when responding to administrative interventions and recommendations.

All in all, in every community, parents and students have a list of teachers whom they would like to avoid at all costs. These teachers simply don't meet the needs of their clientele and are not going to change. Children get hurt, as principals, superintendents, and boards of education are impotent to effect change. Some of the problems lie with administrators who are unwilling to utilize the discipline interventions at their disposal. Most of the blame, however, lies with state governments that have created expensive, unfair labor regulations which allow the practitioners of poor practice to thrive.

Teachers associations are not wrong when they have a lack of trust regarding boards and administrators. Some are mean-spirited leaders who will punish good teachers who do not kiss the administrator's power ring or backside. Additionally, boards of education may go after senior teachers simply because they cost more or give their children a bad grade. As such, any modification of tenure must consider these risk factors and utilize an outside evaluation system prior to dismissal of a tenured individual.

Tenure can be modified in several ways to protect good teachers and children who deserve the best instructors. Our proposal will be added to the many others that are circulating through the present educational dialogue. They include the following:

- Increasing the probationary period prior to tenure to five years.
- Allowing parental and student input to administrators making decisions regarding tenure.
- Having a state panel of administrators available to come in for an outside evaluation of a teacher who receives two negative annual evaluations.
- Including in the state panels review, student input (trusting the evaluators to accurately separate personal issues from negative patterns of behavior).
- Guaranteeing to schools a system which features tenure review, removal from tenure, and appeal processes that are affordable and expedient.
- Mandating training for instructional supervisors and random review by state panels of written administrative lesson evaluations.
- Removing tenure for teachers who *repeatedly* are not selected by a lottery system and/or are poorly rated by students and parents and fail to remediate with administrative intervention.

GOVERNMENT AND SCHOOLS OF EDUCATION

Schools of education are regulated by their home university, which decides on approaches and training. Unfortunately, for many colleges, both cash and students are needed for their very survival. As could be expected under these conditions, standards are minimal and quality is uneven.

Utilizing the undergraduate and graduate education of educators is the best opportunity to improve the quality of education. This book has a central theme of wrong paradigms leading to mistaken decisions, which result in schools that provide less than students and parents want and deserve.

This book challenges the view that student opinions are not worthy and that students' happiness in school is not a key goal of school reform. Being caught in the same paradigm as others, schools of education invariably ignore the concept of student satisfaction and offer few if any classes on relationships and feedback from clients/students. Classes on pedagogy are often a joke as the professor may establish a format for lesson plans, but for the most part, very little is done regarding creating better methods for teaching and teaching new teachers to use best practices for student learning.

Additionally, schools of education rarely insist that prospective teachers be experts on anything. The social studies teacher may not understand history, the math teacher may be a mediocre math student, and so on. Schools of education, for the most part, do not adequately test prospective teachers on the academic subjects they are going to teach.

One impact that government can have on the world of education is to have stronger mandates and controls on schools of education. Government should insist on programs dealing with relationships, crisis management, proven pedagogical practices, and more. Furthermore, state and federal governments can insist on the use of problem-solving models in education classes. It is unfair for a new teacher to be placed blind into difficult situations when they have been poorly trained.

Education classes must give students real-life scenarios and make them consider what option they would take when confronted with a difficult situation. Today, new teachers are being sent out very ill-prepared for what they are about to face in a world more complicated than ever before. Hence, we see tremendous turnover among young teachers fleeing the field, as they were not appropriately prepared to face the classroom realities.

The national teacher examinations are simply operating on too minimal a standard to guarantee that the appropriate people make it into a classroom. Government should insist on a minimum cumulative average for a prospective teacher. Trainees falling short in academic prowess could make it up by tackling more advanced courses.

In summary, this blind neglect regarding the feeder training institutions to the American public schools is inherently damaging. Government must get involved and foster an expectation of excellence in the world of teacher education based on sound processes for finding, preparing, and supporting teachers from initiation to career.

GOVERNMENT AND BAD SCHOOLS

In New York City, schools that are considered failing are closed and the personnel is shuffled to other institutions. This reorganization is a good start but does not go far enough. Urgency on the part of teachers and administrators is important regarding turning around a failed school. If the school closes, and the employee winds up with a transfer to another school, what urgency existed?

In the mid-1990s New York State took over management of the Roosevelt School District on Long Island because of gross mismanagement. The state did a poor job, got caught in overseeing a fiscally unsound program, and has run from any similar action ever since. Unfortunately, some schools and school systems are so mismanaged that failure to assume control is a criminal act of nonfeasance, which is a crime of negligence. Or in other words, a crime is occurring in which the party should have known better—the party being elected representatives and officials of state departments of education.

States must have minimum standards to allow a school or a school district to operate. If the board of education is so inept that the children are being denied an appropriate education, then a failure to act is condoning the reality that many children are being condemned to a substandard life. Children have been told that they can expect protection from the system; but in today's world, none will be coming.

A discussion to close down a substandard school happened recently in Rhode Island. Under Rhode Island law, if this action had been taken, only a certain percentage of the former teachers would have been rehired in the newly created school. Negotiations between the superintendent and the teachers association worked out a compromise, and the crisis was circumvented. Or was it? What about making substantial change for the kids? Likely the compromise was helpful in getting the students extra help, but did it substantially change the education they were receiving? In all likelihood, it is very unlikely; and a substandard school continued to operate, albeit, perhaps a little improved.

The truth is, although a number of schools in every state should be closed, almost none are. There is a phrase regarding tenure: "When in doubt, kick them out." The truth is, when in doubt, almost all teachers make it through to tenure. Well, the truth really is, "Schools in doubt will have no turn about." The school might get a little better, reaching minimal standards, but who wants to send their children to schools that have succeeded in moving up to only minimum standards?

Government has to get tough and close down bad schools. In the time prior to the closing, a team of outside experts can help to determine educators who are part of the problem and educators who are part of the solution. Those educators who are part of the solution should be the first hired in the new institution. Those who are part of the problem should be wished a happy life in another field.

GOVERNMENT AND A STUDENT ADVOCACY BOARD

In the Rhode Island school showdown, the superintendent and the teachers reached a compromise. Of course, absent from all contract discussions were the students and student representatives. Everyone assumed that the superintendent negotiated on behalf of the students. However, the teachers association might have made the same claim, citing failures on the part of the school district. The truth is, no one represented the students.

Thus, in all contract negotiation, educational legislation, and lobbying efforts, one party is always unrepresented: the students. Everyone claims the mantle of speaking on behalf of the students, including the PTA, the school board, superintendents, teachers associations, etc. In this case, "when everyone speaks for you, no one speaks for you." The nearly 50 million students in the public schools are the greatest unrepresented minority in the United States.

A solution for the "powerlessness of students" would be for government to create a Student Advocacy Board (SAB) whose only job would be to consider the needs of the students. Contracts would need to be reviewed by the SAB, legislation would be commented on by the SAB, and funding inequities would need to be reviewed by the SAB. The more authority and power an SAB was given, the more schools would improve.

Another big misconception in public education is that children from advantaged neighborhoods who do well in school are also being well treated in school. Not necessarily. Of course these types of fancy schools have principals and teachers who do treat students well; however, these schools may have educators who are substandard but are being protected by the strong student performance.

Not only does the state leave these educators alone, but also the *children* who desire favorable grades and recommendations for college know it is best to not challenge their poor treatment and the substandard education offered by individual teachers. Their parents figure this out as well. For now, the solution has been for their parents to hire tutors to fill in for the lack of appropriate teaching. And of course, the bad educator takes credit for the work of the tutored child. Thus, an SAB would be a good solution for identifying and helping students who are being mistreated or undereducated in advantaged communities.

The government has decided that education today is about standardized assessments. More than a decade into the movement, do students now feel that standardized tests are improving their education? Do students want teachers to be reviewed by outside evaluators or do they trust principals and chairpeople? Does their high school give them appropriate guidance on the college admissions process and/or job placements? To what extent do students feel that their school treats them well? Are students respected as people?

Do teachers who make over $100,000 a year refuse to give extra help? *Tell it to the Student Advocacy Board*! Empower the SAB to review a contract, or an action of the state education department; or better yet, recommend the closing of a school . . . real change in real time!

Students have a right to a voice—and many traditional institutions that have maintained that they speak for the children have lied. So institute real change in real time by empowering a Student Advocacy Board!

GOVERNMENT AND A PHILOSOPHY STATEMENT

Americans have always wondered about the real purpose of the public schools. Various eras in American history have come up with a variety of philosophies. Usually the social, political, or economic fears of the day helped shape the philosophy that the public blindly accepted.

Government fears have included the Americanization of immigrants, the communist threat, the brainwashing of American prisoners of war (POWs) in Korea, the launch of *Sputnik*, the desegregation of the public schools, the teenage protests of the Vietnam War, and more. Today, the fear is mainly an economic one. Invariably, when someone is referring to the failure of the American public schools to educate appropriately, the banner line is attached that we must be wary of "our future way of life" being threatened because our children are undereducated and ill-prepared to compete in a world economy.

Government can do a major service for the future generations of children by creating an educational philosophy for the public schools that is sensible—and then sticking with it for multiple generations. Americans want for their public schools what they want for their own children. We want our children to live with joy and peace and to learn advanced skills.

We seek to make our children able and willing to apply their knowledge to the betterment of others and to create a life in which economic problems are absent. We want our children to live lives that are meaningful and to bring honor to themselves, their home, and their community.

As a result of the absence of a national philosophy, today we consider successful schooling a good score on a minimum competency (and often unfair) standardized test. So this is our philosophy of education: All American children will do well on minimum competency tests—and we wonder why so many schools are a mess?

SUMMARY

Kids need the government to get it right. The power of government for good can be unparalleled, just as the power of government to do damage is also unparalleled. Today's interventions regarding standardized tests are beset with terrible side effects, not the least of which is an attack on the free-thinking model that has contributed to Americans being able to think out of the box for generations. If government continues to operate with inappropriate interventions, the American public schools are doomed to more generations of mediocrity.

Chapter Five

Screwed-Up by Clueless Boards of Education and Misguided Parent Groups

Despite two decades of a "national effort" to intervene in the public schools, American education, for the most part, is still a local affair. The power to set tax rates, approve books, create a district's goals, and write its mission statement have been the business of the local board of education.

CLUELESS BOARDS OF EDUCATION

In composition, boards of education today are not very different from their counterparts in the nineteenth century. At that time, the men in authority in the community would come together and form a board of education, often consisting of the local minister, a shop keeper, a banker, and the wealthiest land owner. At its inception, the board would then run the entire school system, a task not difficult given that most early schools had only one room with one teacher, the classic "one-room schoolhouse."

However, as communities grew bigger, schools became more populated and required services that had outgrown the volunteer board's ability to manage. At that point, boards of education began hiring chief operating officers for their schools, who came with a variety of titles such as superintendent, district principal, or simply principal. Today, the practices of a local governing board—i.e., overseeing local education—are in their third century in the United States.

So the question now arises: How well has the system of local governance of schools worked? Are we satisfied with our local schools and their ability to educate our children? Do students and parents regale us with tales of how their lives were changed for the better as a result of the actions of the local school board? And, if we wish to apply the twenty-first century standards of accountability, to what degree has the local school board accepted responsibility for the failures of the school system they oversee when they occur?

TODAY'S SITUATION

In actuality, the local school boards have successfully situated themselves in a position of virtual non-accountability. Although they are in charge of hiring the superintendent, deciding on the school district's budget, and determining where the money goes, school boards have succeeded in not taking the blame for the problems of schooling. In fact, the lack of accountability of local school boards in the face of a perpetual crisis in education is staggering.

For a moment, to narrow the scope of reviewing school boards, we might consider one particular role of the system. How successfully have school boards created educational opportunity, equality, and quality within the schools they oversee? To most, the answer is obvious, based on our perpetual effort to fix schools: not very well.

Interestingly, as schools fail across the country with an outcry for greater accountability, boards of education have come under little to no scrutiny.

In fact, in recently enacted legislation in New York State to improve schools through accountability, school boards were simply ignored as the new review system holds principals and teachers accountable for student outcomes on a strict performance basis. The New York accountability system, which ignores the role of the board of education, is not the exception in twenty-first-century school governance; it is the rule around the country.

No Child Left Behind, Race to the Top, and the latest account-ability reforms were designed as if school boards were not players in the educational system. Clearly, state legislators wanted to ig-nore the powerful role that school boards play in creating the chaos—and at times the success—that has evolved within schools. As Shear reported:

> I attended a conference in which a retired superintendent from a district which had superlative gains was speaking. I cornered him during a coffee break and said, "How did you ever get some of the reforms you enacted past your board of education? In retrospect, they worked, but one would think that the board would have never allowed some of them." The retired superin-tendent looked up, laughed and said, "I never told them. Wouldn't it be great if there were no boards of education?"

Curiously, boards have been left unaccountable regardless of how badly their schools are doing. A school system can underperform for decades, and the board is never called to task. It can hire district superintendents and fire them, owe them back pay, and not be held accountable. A board can create a non-productive, non-educational climate and not even be questioned. The truth is, the system has allowed boards to operate in a screwed-up manner for so long that screwed-up has become the norm.

Arguably, boards are considered macro-policy creators with specific fiduciary requirements. Their job is not to manage intricate educational policy or get into schools' daily operations. However, that illusion has sailed out the window with state and national board associations calling for greater and greater board intervention into the academics of schooling. School board conventions often look for transformational practices that board members can learn about and bring back to their school districts. However, the reality is, board members do get involved, do demand administrators and teachers buckle to their wishes, and are involved in education on a micro-level.

In most cases, no group is as powerful—and at the same time as clueless in the area of schooling—as boards of education. Individual board members across the country can articulate quite well their perceptions of what is wrong; but for the most part, they have not offered effective remedies. In the overwhelming percentage of cases, board members are ill-prepared for the major job they have undertaken. As such, new board members quickly either adopt the "company line" or become the loyal (or disloyal) opposition. Rarely if ever do board members call for real discussions of the foundation concepts driving their school system, with the possible exception of how money is spent.

In fairness, we must point out that boards have been called upon to expand their traditional areas of responsibility, as society has grown increasingly less trustful of professional educators and their ability to effect positive change. However, since board members are untrained in the field of policy-making in education, they are less likely than professional educators to understand some of the traps of the present-day educational reform movement.

One of the problems with board intervention in school operations and classroom teaching is that school board members often do not know what will make schools better. As a result, members have fallen into the national trap that increased accountability testing will reverse the national education crisis. In the present incarnation of school reform, board members have been seduced by the latest educational fad—that all things can be solved with better accountability for educators. Of course, the accountability has to be based on something—and student results on standardized tests have become the litmus test for good schools.

The reality of accountability testing is that outcomes are closely tied to socioeconomic conditions. Boards from lower socioeconomic communities usually have far more urgent issues than fourth-grade English Language Arts test results. On the other hand, board members from more advantaged districts have time to review standardized test results as if they were looking at the baseball standings. A Long Island elementary principal explained,

> We did pretty well in Nassau County on the Elementary ELA tests but the following year we had a few ELL families move into our community. The kids did not speak English, yet the state still demanded they take the test. Obviously, they were below standards and it dropped our school performance by a few percentage points as we have a small school population. The Board of Education screamed about the results in a public meeting. They never asked why our passing percentage went down a few points.

As a result of the embracing of quality through standardized tests, as stated in earlier chapters, the accountability movement will not only fail to solve educational problems, but will also make things worse as it does not address the foundation issues of schooling that have caused the problem. So what should board members do? How can they use their power to fix a system that hurts children? How do they use their power so that their schools get better?

These are complicated problems for a poorly trained elected group of local citizens. So perhaps a good place to start is with the area of board training. A mother explained:

In my community the president of the board of education was the receptionist at my dentist's office. She is a nice lady and polite, but she doesn't even have a college degree. Aren't there rules for who can serve on a board? Aren't there requirements of some sort?

In response an assistant superintendent stated:

There are very few rules for who can sit on a board of education and what knowledge they must possess. In fact, the entire accountability of the board is left up to the voter at the ballot box. Voters who will vote for their friend or the person who helped them get the teacher they wanted for their child.

One of the traditional roles of board members is to watch over the finances of the district. All too often, they aren't even very good at doing this traditional role of being the fiduciary watch dogs. In Roslyn, New York, for example, board members were blind for years to an embezzling scheme enacted by the superintendent, assistant superintendent for business, and a clerk in the business office. After the conviction of the three, the state of New York responded with a demand that board members take a finance course regarding school management.

However, while the state acknowledged that boards need better training on money matters, the state has ignored that boards also need better training on their other responsibilities regarding educational policies and programs.

Obviously it is crucial that a board of education know how to raise and spend money wisely. In this area, unbelievably, a simple matrix is not being used to determine where monies are spent, comparing districts. How much one district spends on classroom instruction, administration, books, extracurricular activities, science research programs, etc., should be based on a district's stated fiduciary philosophy (see Cooper, 2001).

That districts do not compare exactly where their money is spent, in comparison to other districts, is the height of irresponsibility! These data are something the states can be contracted to provide for districts, as Rhode Island and South Carolina do using In$ite, a finance analysis model. Comparative evaluations will go a long way to seeing that monies are better spent on behalf of children. But unfortunately, funds are not always spent on the direct teaching of children, with real resources reaching the classroom for direct instruction of children. Shear stated:

> I was told by the business administrator in March that our budget was now frozen and I couldn't spend any more money even if it was in my budget. She told me this included student field trips. When I announced this to my faculty they went nuts because the Board of Education was planning a trip to the National School Board Convention being held in California. I didn't know about the board trip but when all hell broke loose, I was the one who was held accountable for the problem. The superintendent demanded to know why I told the faculty that the budget was frozen. When I told her that they would notice when I cancelled all field trips, she just got madder.

The other major role that is traditionally reserved for the board of education is the hiring and reviewing of the superintendent. Board members involved in hiring their superintendent are, for the most part, ignorant of the system or game in which superintendents get hired. The present system of success in American school leadership rests on making as few enemies as possible. Thus, a certain type of candidate emerges when boards are looking for a superintendent: one who has not shaken things up very much in the past.

Hiring and Change

When hiring a leader, board attitudes can be contrary to the interests of students and the best means of improving their schools. Today's hiring methods are dominated by two practices: promoting internal candidates and conducting a comprehensive search. Internal promotions are interesting in that the real change agents whom so many districts desire are often eliminated when districts consider hiring from within. If districts have a real change agent within their district, the person has invariably made significant decisions that people disagree with. People hate change and educators hate change more than most (see Carlson, 1962).

A district's internal change agent has probably stepped on toes and frightened some local people, as internal change agents make powerful enemies within the administrative community of principals and chairpeople. Many school administrators are committed more to the status quo than they would ever realize. Boards when hiring must consider whether the internal candidate may also be the person who did what is best for children when hearing negative reviews.

New paradigm: When considering an internal candidate, be wary of the enemies that line up against the candidate. They may in fact be the bad guys, although they may have a nice smile and a charming wit.

The second popular way to hire a superintendent is by conducting a search. In many cases, boards hire a consultant who is either a large search firm or a small local group. In both cases, these groups are often dominated by former superintendents. Be aware that they like their own and will give undue preference to recycling colleagues who are inclined to favor the status quo.

Individuals who do not fit the traditional paradigm of a superintendent will struggle for acceptance by the "old guard." Additionally, some search firms will work on stealing superintendents from other districts. In the short run, this move costs both districts money as it drives salaries upward.

The school board that engages a firm to recruit another district's leader probably needs to reconsider the practice, as we invariably place an undue halo on the head of the recruited one. We love what we can't have or when we think we can outsmart the next guy in a neighboring district. High-end search firms can charge districts over $20,000 and then recruit and steal candidates to justify their high price tag. A district that spends that much money is likely to be set up in one way or another.

When boards are doing any level of hiring, a healthy degree of suspicion must be exercised in considering references. People will say nice things about people who have earned it, and they will say nice things about people whom they are anxious to dump. As a school board member explained:

> I was a new school board member and the existing board members had agreed not to do back channel reference checks in our superintendent search. As a result, when a board member I knew from the district "dumping the superintendent we were hiring" said to me, "Watch your pockets," my colleagues didn't want to hear any of it. As the board member from the other district had predicted, the major initiative the superintendent created over the next 6 years was to raise his own salary. He was quite good at it.

When a school board uses a third party to conduct a search, a new set of interests enter the picture. Remember in this situation that the third party is a business that has a different set of goals than the school district. Although apparently the search firm wants to find the client district a suitable superintendent, in fact, they simply want to find a superintendent. In one recent case on Long Island, after the consultant failed to find a suitable candidate, he offered himself as an interim superintendent.

This action, of course, was a clear conflict of interest. But the truth is, school boards must be careful when using a search firm, as a former superintendent stated:

> Of course there was no reference check; the guy was an old friend of the retired superintendent doing the search. When he got the job, he was a multi-year disaster and the district was

gun-shy about hiring another superintendent following this
mess. As a result, they went to a number of interims before
actually hiring a new superintendent. In fact, the guy doing the
search never did reference checks—he recommended his
friends.

It is always best to hear from as many people as possible who know
the candidate. The more insight a board member can have regarding the next school leader to be hired, the better. New paradigm:
Boards need to trust their own instincts and do their own research
when hiring a superintendent. Checking on a school leader, in addition to what a search firm and references provide, is a must!

A NEW ROLE FOR PARENTS

While local school board roles are traditionally held by parents, the
job of a school board member requires a professional restraint that
may not be in the best interests of children. The same protocol for
candor within the school system does not exist within the parental
community.

Many parents are very knowledgeable about their school district,
after their child has gone through the system. As explained by an
elementary principal:

> The fascinating thing about parents is that they have an opinion
> about every teacher in my building . . . and they are right about
> every teacher in my building.

Among the problems that parents have is that other parents, who
evidence inappropriate behavior, frequently shape the face of the
parental community to educators. As a result, educators have become very good at circling the wagons to keep parents at bay, or
simply to get them to go away. Parents need to recognize what is
appropriate and inappropriate in their dealings with school offi-

cials. Adding to this dilemma is that "what is appropriate is often in the eye of the beholder." That being said, parental communities will be empowered by rallying around the coherent and appropriate. The lack of an effective parental voice in the dialogue of school change has allowed practices that are harmful to children to become routine.

Parents in elementary schools in many communities have an excellent idea of which teachers they would like to teach their children, and which teachers they would like to have their children avoid. Of course, the administration in most places won't let parents choose which teacher their child will have for a course or a year of school. But it is a pretty safe bet that in a school with multiple teachers on each grade level, the board member and the PTA president's child will not wind up in the classroom of the nasty, screaming teacher whom every knowledgeable parent is trying to avoid.

In most school districts, the uninvolved parents are more likely to have their children get the problem teachers on the elementary level. However, depending on the size of the district, by the time the child reaches high school, he or she is often treated more equitably, depending on the school administration. This change does not occur because schools have become more benevolent; it happens because of the difficulty in maneuvering schedules at the high school level. One persistent factor is that dissatisfied parents, regardless of how accurate their observations may be, seem impotent in protecting their children from incompetent teachers.

New paradigm: Parental complaints in the form of not wanting their child to have a particular teacher should be registered and recorded. Additionally, teachers have gone to great lengths to protect themselves from anonymous complaints. Although fair, this namelessness does not deal with the reality that parents are often afraid that a complaint will do nothing but hurt their children. A formula should be enacted by which at a reasonable point the teacher is placed on probation and ultimately let go if over a period of time enough parents say they do *not* want their child in that teacher's class.

Parents should not be the chief evaluator of teachers. However, parents should not be disenfranchised from the process either. We must stress being reasonable and also ensuring that the unfavorable review is held equally with that of the administration and that the educator has been given a significant (but not unending) chance to improve.

Additionally, parents whose children are graduating should be able to register thoughts about their child's experience, following their school completion. The review system also has to identify problem parents who complain, bully, and harass their child's teachers on a regular basis. This process of appropriate registering of parent opinions will only be successful if it is also fair. *This process should not be a free swing at dedicated educators by inappropriate parents.* If the system does not protect the appropriate teacher and single out the inappropriate actions, the system will do far more harm than good.

Parent Advocacy Board

Part of the problem in American education is that parents have accepted that mediocre is better than bad. Therefore, the concept that a parent will be able to send their child to a superior school is frequently missing from the dialogue. As one parent of an elementary student said:

> I asked a friend I met in the PTA about the schools. She said they are OK for public schools. I was a bit confused, but after having my son in the schools for a period of years, if someone asked me how are the schools?—I would say they are OK for public schools.

Parents have also hit a stone wall in their knowledge and ability to change a school system for which they are paying. Educators are good at "circling the wagons" as contracts have taken precedence over children's needs. Parents are told that extra help is limited, communication is poor, and their ability to steer their child through the matrix of the school system is limited. Too many parents are dissatisfied customers who would not come back if they had another option.

Parents who go up against educators are frequently isolated and out-gunned. Further compounding the problem is that their complaints will die in the ears of most school leaders who believe they are stuck with the bad educator. Thus, a combination of bad principals, an ineffective central office, and a benign school board can institutionalize bad practice and the hurting of children.

Each district should have a Parent Advocacy Board (PAB) whose members would be professionally trained to consider carefully the difference between an appropriate complaint and an inappropriate parent who is out of line. The PAB will soon come to learn who are the weaker teachers and administrators, and will understand who the children are who make the lives of other children more difficult. The PAB will send an advocate/representative with a parent when they are dealing with a teacher, principal, or both. Many parents don't realize they are walking into a virtual ambush when they come to school to lodge a complaint.

For many principals, the backing of a teacher, even when they are wrong, can be in the principal's best interest in numerous ways. Backing a parent complaint can have numerous negative side effects for a school administrator. Given the uneven playing field, parents need to know what they are dealing with when they meet with a teacher. As a middle-school parent said:

> My brother, who was a teacher at the time but later went on to be a principal, gave me a heads up when I was going to meet with my daughter's 7th-grade math teacher. He told me that I

would probably meet with the teacher and her advocate. I had just expected to meet with the teacher and talk about my daughter's progress in her math class. My brother schooled me on how to handle the meeting, what I wanted out of the meeting and how to follow up. I am in finance, and it was incredible how much I didn't know about how to handle the school system. Sure enough, I walked into an ambush. Luckily, I had been prepped.

A PAB would have the opportunity to help orient and prepare parents on appropriate ways to lodge a complaint and ask for action. The PAB could register complaints and differentiate between a teacher who has repeated complaints from a widespread number of sources, over a period of years, and a situation in which one parent is trying to create a witch hunt against an individual teacher or is a malcontent who is always unhappy and is constantly lodging a complaint.

The PAB could also monitor the administration's effectiveness with issues of bullying, discipline, and safety, working with the administration to examine concerns such as homework, which, depending upon the student's learning track, is frequently too much or too little. In fact, the PAB can help see that the administration does its job of educational oversight and improvement.

Quite frankly, the limited role of parents in monitoring and affecting their child's school is incredible. Although there are many inappropriate parents, we must remember that the vast majority are accurate in their evaluation of their child's education and desire for better schools. Children are screwed-up by their parents having a limited role in the public schools. A system in which effective feedback can be provided and processed is desirable and will result in institutional improvement.

National Organizations

Parent groups in the form of the National Parent Teacher Association (PTA) and school boards in the form of the National School Board Association are both missing golden opportunities to be more effective. While both groups make positive contributions, apparently they are quite unaware of their potential power and the opportunity they have to help the "screwed-up" condition that children endure in many schools.

Both organizations attempt to be nonpolitical in a political world. In fact, these organizations need to take a position and advocate rules that are pro-student and pro-parent. For example, state tenure laws for teachers and administrators, which protect the inappropriate, are clearly the outgrowth of strong political and union organizations advocating on the part of teachers.

The time has come for strong political organizations, speaking for the rights of parents and students, effectively to lobby for pro-student rule changes. State legislatures will listen to parents on issues of health, nutrition, and safety. However, parental advocacy for educational protection against incompetence is missing from the legislative dialogue. It is time for that to change.

Parents and Accountability

Parents and school board members have bought into the rhetoric that good schools have high test scores. Even statistically reliable and valid testing is subjective, being based on a number of factors such as quality of prior teaching, alignment of curriculum with the assessment, quality of school management, parental involvement, conditions in which the children sit for the test, experiential knowledge possessed by the children, socioeconomic status of the student population, prior education of the ESL population, special education numbers, and much more.

If the list of variables affecting student outcomes on standard-ized assessments seems overwhelming, one also has to recognize that this listing is still incomplete. The number of variables that might explain why a child does well or poorly on a standardized assessment is staggering. Yet, the conventional wisdom of American decision-makers is that the assessments can be used to measure teacher performance.

Compounding the problem, these variables are dependent on statistically reliable and valid assessments over a period of time. Standardized tests by their very nature are extremely difficult to make statistically reliable and valid when they attempt accurately to measure growth across years for millions of different children.

Not surprisingly, tests across the country have been problematic and have failed in accurately identifying where the gaps are in educational preparation for individual children. Not the least of these problems is that the movement over the last decade called for standards but not a clearly delineated curriculum. As such, educa-tors have had trouble aligning curriculum with the assessment; and many districts are too overwhelmed to work effectively on this alignment. Assessments, which are non-aligned with the actual cur-riculum that the children are taught, are inaccurate measures of performance, as stated by an assistant superintendent in New York State to Shear:

> The state assessments are a joke. Assistant Superintendents for Curriculum try to guess which textbook or learning series from which company bests aligns with the state test. All too often, we do not know exactly what will be on the test, so how do you prepare your students? Additionally, each year the state changes the passing score. So the local papers will post a comparison of annual scores without telling the public that the passing score changed. And for high performing small districts, one family of ESL children who move in and must sit for the assessment can bring your score down several percent.

Again leaving you constantly on the defensive. When you go to a board meeting and get attacked because the district dropped 3% in grade 4 from the prior year—and you know it is a different cohort of kids, it is pretty hard to not be demoralized. What results is a narrowing of curriculum and enrichment to teach to the test. This teaching to the test model is screwing up our kids' education—big time!

The new "Common Core" is meant to help this alignment process. However, what adds to the lack of credibility of the government is that they have gone so long without realizing and adjusting the standards into a "real curriculum." The amazing fact is that parents have allowed this to happen to their children. Schools are being run outside the realm of plain common sense and practical improvement.

For example, parents who have several children know that each child walked, talked, and progressed at different times and at different rates. We do not develop according to a chronological time clock exactly as a book or an expert would predict. We all progress at different rates. The entire accountability system is based on children chronologically developing at the same exact speed to the same level; this is a flawed concept.

The downside to forcing children to read *before* they are developmentally ready can be devastating and is a major contributor to the high special-education numbers. This problem is especially true for boys, who are often developmentally behind girls at the same chronological age.

When parents and school board members allow this false parameter of success to creep into the system, terrible outcomes often result. Districts will do everything in their power to pick up test scores while everything else suffers. When test assessments are done well, they can be an important variable in showing weaknesses and strengths in curriculum or pedagogy. The problem is

that many of the assessments are not done well, are out of alignment with the curriculum, and are frequently used as the single
variable indicating an excellent or poor school system or teacher.

What parents want from schools is not a complicated question;
yet it has *not been* the driving force of the parental community. Too
often, parents have taken a back seat and allowed schools to operate
in violation of their child's basic human rights. Parents want their
children to have the best possible experience while in school and
the best possible opportunities as a result of their schooling. They
want their children to be able to come out of school with the ability
to compete successfully in a twenty-first-century environment.
They want their children to have their character and humanity enhanced.

Do results on a standardized test really help students to compete
in a world economy and act as ethical members of society? Of
course the answer is no. And again, the problem is that schools do
not operate the way they should because schools have not been
designed with the correct foundation principles. In the case of what
parents want for their children, the foundation must be centered on
love. We want the people our children meet in school to greet them
and treat them with love and caring. Parents and grandparents want
schools that operate on a central theme of love. They want schools
that have high expectations and high support for their children.

Parents must create their own checklist for improvement. However, the authors of this publication are more than willing to provide parents with a matrix of options to consider. They include
advocating and implementing through governmental pressure the
following changes:

1. Selecting schools and classes through a lottery system based
   on market choice.
2. Creating a market-driven accountability system in which educators with a bottom rating year after year must improve or be
   replaced.

3. Replacing chronologically based assessments with developmentally based approaches, including the creation of an extended kindergarten experience for children not ready to progress into the first grade.

4. Giving educators an avenue for effective parent assessment, since educators are witnesses to abusive, absentee, and ineffective parenting. Additionally, inappropriate parents frequently attempt to hold educators responsible for their poor parenting. Appropriate parents must circumvent the damage that inappropriate parents do to the system.

5. Insisting that schools are based on concepts of love and not on accountability based on standardized testing.

6. Uniting advocates for their children when budgetary cuts are considered by state legislatures.

7. Training boards of education with a mandatory standard for clarification of their role and better tools to hire and evaluate the superintendent.

8. Holding boards of education and superintendents accountable for school systems in which parents and students are largely dissatisfied based on market research.

9. Making the state and national PTA and School Board Association a more serious voice for children and parents.

10. Establishing local advocacy boards to articulate the problems of a system since parents are afraid to come forward and reveal their concerns.

SUMMARY

Parents have inherently squandered away their oversight of and responsibility for their children's education in America. This failure on the part of parents to be "effective"—in providing their children with the type of education and experience that the parents would have wanted for their children—is among the main reasons that America's public school students attend school in "screwed-up" circumstances.

Parents have enormous power when that power is used by a group with a clear agenda of "what is in the best interest of children" at the heart of its advocacy. If schools are to improve, parents simply have to be better at forcing the type of change that is necessary to create the schools they desire for their children.

Chapter Six

School Funding Is Screwed-Up

Arguably, one of the biggest problems facing school board members, their districts, and therefore their children in the twenty-first century is their constant need and inability to raise and use funds effectively and efficiently to improve student learning. Traditional education funding formulas and practices have created an American school system that is inherently inequitable, inefficient, ineffective—and costly.

Education consumes the third highest percentage and amount of public spending in the United States, as shown in table 5.1. Of the $6.1 trillion spent on government functions, we see education costing $0.9 trillion in 2011.

We know that education is important and that the federal, state, and local governments share an interest in and support of the largest public enterprise (with nearly 56 million children and 6 million adults involved daily in K–12 public and private education). Thus, for all the money and effort, we realize that schools could do better and be of higher quality in meeting the needs of all children and preparing them for a productive life by using public dollars more efficiently and equitably.

Table 6.1. Total Government Spending in the United States Federal, State, and Local Fiscal Year 2011

Government Pensions	$1.0 trillion
Government Health Care	+$1.1 trillion
K-12 Education Spending	+$.09 trillion
National Defense	+$1.0 trillion
Government Welfare	+$0.6 trillion
All Other Spending	+$1.5 trillion
Total Government Spending	+$6.1 trillion
Federal Deficit	+$1.6 trillion

Efforts to overcome these problems have occupied educators, policy-makers, and economists for centuries. As Berne and Stiefel (1999, p. 7) explained:

> The idea of "America as a land of opportunity" captures an essential part of our national spirit and heritage—and public education is often viewed as the institution that can transform this ideal into a reality. Thus, an equitable system of education is one that offsets those accidents of birth that keep some children from having an opportunity to function fully in the economic and political life of the community.

State governments have acknowledged these financial and legal problems, with numerous school equity court cases and attempts to fix the system in court and state legislatures almost every year. As mentioned in chapter 4, New York classifies "similar schools" based on the resources of the schools' districts. Acknowledging lower expectations for schools in high poverty areas, New York State has not only institutionalized inequitable school funding, but has also used rankings as part of its rating system.

Given the economic constraints that American society is facing, new financial answers for schools are needed today, now more than ever. We hope that the concepts we are about to offer will not only save taxpayers money, but will also allow for a good if not a better education for all children.

These new concepts include a wide range of changes, such as major structural alterations in government as well as other innovations in K–12 education, new approaches to athletics, lower teaching and administrative salaries, federal tax relief for educators on pensions, reduced local taxes, and reduced state taxes. And we have some real reforms in teacher reimbursement separate from salary, including reduced higher education costs for graduate school, faculty housing, and college tuition relief for faculty children. We also recommend utilization of a better system for centralized services, differentiated medical care for faculty, and a lecture hall approach to certain situations.

We see the need, too, for revisions of the middle school model, new approaches to the special education services, busing, custodial services, and ancillary services that are different in each district, and more. These ideas can be controversial; and we know from experience that proposed change will be attacked even when the status quo is unacceptable. As such, these ideas are for public discussion, and we hope they will contribute to new paradigms in the areas of school financing.

We recognize systemic, large-scale national problems with the U.S. funding of K–12 public schools. Many of these difficulties have grown and increased over the last fifty years, challenging the structure, operations, and quality of American education. We need to take the immediate steps that schools can take to make the system more efficient and effective, if done properly.

Idea 1—*Do away with the middle schools*. The abolition of the middle school has already begun in many parts of the country. The important thing is that educational reformers can learn from studying the debacle of the middle school. Middle schools were developed in the 1970s, with two major purposes: to improve educational outcomes and to accommodate the emotional and social needs of emerging adolescents. Apparently, middle schools (and junior high schools earlier) were accomplishing neither—not improving outcomes or meeting the needs of pre- and early adolescents—but middle school advocates dug in, and the movement has gone on for close to two decades after it could reasonably be concluded that the concept did not work. Additionally, many implementation strategies for the middle school movement dramatically drove up the cost of schooling with virtually nothing to show for it.

In some variations of middle schools, teachers involved in a teaming structure often taught their fifth class as an enrichment in order to make a four-person team work. Other variations took away teachers from hall duty and cafeteria duty. Schools then had to hire aides at additional cost. Additionally, the aides simply could not handle many of the problems in middle school cafeterias and hallways. Therefore, the model required greater administrative presence in the cafeteria that took school leaders away from more important tasks such as supervision of instruction.

The abolition of the middle school movement and replacement of it with a different system that does provide students with additional support will save money and personnel resources. Depending on the model, it may save a little money or a substantial amount.

Idea 2—*Stop paying for non-academic programs and let the community take them over*. Do the models of the Boy Scouts, Girl Scouts and the local Little League really work? If so, how about the next idea? Today, American schools offer a wide array of athletic and cocurricular activities financed by school budgets. Arguably these expenditures are very important as these programs keep kids busy in worthwhile activities under adult supervision. The question is, Does the taxpayer want to pay for it?

The mission of the public schools is not to be baby sitters or to keep kids busy in worthwhile activity following their school day. However, many social and athletic services have been assigned to our schools over the decades. And schools do this mission extremely well.

We are not advocating that communities allow their kids to have free time after school in unsupervised situations. In fact, we think that is often a very bad idea. However, in a financial sense, who pays for it, how it is paid for, and how it is structured should be discussed. The optimum word is *community* rather than *school*, and the ultimate question is finance.

Should communities set up athletic programs and cocurricular activities in towns and counties rather than leaving it to the local school district? Could communities run these programs more efficiently at a lower cost? Based on the concept of volunteerism—probably. It is very unlikely that the programs will be run as well or as professionally, and that is something that must be considered. However, in an era of economic crisis, this concept is one to discuss. A note of caution: the authors believe strongly in investing in children and are not recommending that this concept of economics be implemented. However, in our desire to be honest, we will bring forward various cost-cutting options—even ones we do not always agree with or like.

Idea 3—*New compensation to attract and retain talented educators.* American education needs new avenues of compensation in place of local-tax-generated funds. The salaries for teachers and administrators are the vast majority of every school district's budget. Over the past thirty years, salaries for teachers and administrators have increased as the economy has progressed. Today, the economy has once again turned school districts into cash-reduced entities.

Importantly, educators should be provided with reasonable compensation to meet their economic needs. Additionally, a somewhat competitive environment for attracting individuals to the field not only needs to be retained, it also needs to be enhanced. However, a lower salary does not have to mean reduced compensation.

To attract the best and brightest to the field of education, society must consider a series of alternative compensation programs for educators. The basic concept for reducing cost is having the power of the state and federal government involved in the initiatives. In addition, a coalition of districts funding projects through bonds could ultimately produce a higher quality of education at a dramatically reduced cost.

The projects include condominiums built for educators; free or greatly reduced tuition to state universities for the children of educators (or the equivalent money follows the child to a private institution); reduced federal taxation of educator pensions; reduced federal and state taxes for active educators; high-quality, state-funded health facilities for educators; affordable quality child care; and stores created with reduced prices specifically for educators based on the model utilized for military families.

The basic concept is that if society can provide educators with relief from their major, long-term economic worries, then lower salaries and pensions could become an acceptable reality.

Idea 4—*Use the best teachers to teach the most students*. Reality-based pedagogy needs to be utilized. Many classes are taught by educators in a lecture format, a very common pedagogy as students progress into high school. A better form of education is to allow students to attend a large-room lecture by a top teacher. New ideas and concepts can be presented.

Then, the students can meet at subsequent times with other teachers and aides to work on the concepts presented. Arguably, this approach will be a more effective method of teaching, and it will also have the ability to cut costs.

Idea 5—*Have students pitch in to serve and maintain their own schools in pride.* Students can and should actively help to maintain their school's environment. Perhaps few places reveal the flaws in our culture as clearly as schools that ask our children to do virtually nothing to help maintain their own schools.

Students do not empty garbage cans, clean floors, or wipe off desks, and frequently have to be cajoled to pick up their own mess after lunch. They need to be utilized in maintenance, cleaning, and carpentry within their own school, a process that is great for value and reducing costs.

After all, children's schools are like their homes, and children should come to love them, participate in serving and helping their schools, and growing in these skills. Schools have vocational classes, but rarely do the students get to practice their skills in maintaining and improving their own environment. Back in the nineteenth century, parents often helped to build their community's schools and keep them up. Why not engage the family in fixing and improving their own schools? So, rather than abusing and trashing their schools, students and their parents could help to improve and maintain them.

Idea 6—*Transport students to and from school inexpensively and equitably.* Busing services cost many districts a great deal of money. The state needs to help with transportation costs instead of mandating the problems. For example, some communities have buses that are running with small student loads as a result of high parental pick-ups and drop-offs.

New York State has often refused to allow districts to reduce operating costs, just in case all the kids decide to take the bus one day. In those cases, allow districts to come up with an alternative plan, but reducing transportation costs is an important thing to consider.

Idea 7—*Reduce school heating and cooling costs.* A federal grant could help to convert all school buildings to natural gas, a process that would be good for America and would cut costs dramatically. Overall it would make schools more comfortable, and more economical.

MOVING AHEAD NOW!

Ultimately, boards of education have a primary role in dealing with taxes and funding for schools in many communities. We must decide how best to utilize resources on behalf of children. Accepting the status quo is simply no longer acceptable.

Fund Children, Not Systems

Already, we see that funding education from the top—from the state and school board "down" to the school—doesn't work as well as putting the resources at the school and classroom level and letting the demand bubble up to the systemic level. One of the biggest screw-ups in educational finance is the funding of *systems* and not *children*. We see that school bureaucracies budget from the top, putting money into the system, without driving the funds to the students via their classrooms, teachers, materials, equipment, and technology.

Working to fix that top-down approach, we are recommending a model for "funding the child" through market choice. Parents and children apply to the school they wish, and if one particular school continually has low consumer support, it closes. Focusing on the child—and not "the system"—could break up the bureaucracy, get money to the child, and empower families to enroll their children in the best schools available.

Local Funding, Local Differences

The United States has long lived with local funding differences, based on local property values (land, houses, businesses, industry), that vary greatly from community to community. We need to recognize that we are one nation, one large economy, and are moving into a postindustrial, high-tech world. Schools need to change in the future and their funding must follow. Money should be equitable and flexible, not bureaucratic and monochromatic.

Students' needs, interests, ages, and future are not the same. Why not weight the amount these schools and teachers receive and see that resources reach the school and classroom where the student is living and receiving his or her education? This "pushing funds down to the classroom" would enable our schools to provide the education that children want and need, lessening the controls and bureaucratic structure of schools. Again, with all things in the area of school funding, let reasonableness be our guide.

SUMMARY AND CONCLUSIONS

Many believe, that, in comparison to other countries, the United States spends the most money on the education of our children. This statement is usually prefaced with an explanation that funding alone hasn't solved the problems of education in the United States, and thus we see a very low correlation between more funding and higher, more successful school outcomes.

However, the statement ignores the reality that funds are so often spent on systems, materials, and management functions, all of which make so little real difference in directly helping children. For example, districts often have to fund the turnover of books and curriculum based on continuously changing state mandates and worn out tomes.

The reality further ignores the burden that un/under-funded state, federal and court mandates have placed on school districts. Often, too, the courts have shifted the cost of maintaining a medically needy child, while in school, to the local school district. Formerly, these expenses would have been the responsibility of insurance companies and/or other governmental agencies.

Schools allocate funds based on their cultural history and norms—or in other words, the way "we have always done it." How money is really spent, is almost never revisited and improved. For example, in most cases, districts will have a football team even if they cannot afford remedial reading teachers or science equipment. In short, funding will follow the values of a community, regardless of whether its in the best interest of children.

We know that funding of American schools is inequitable, based on local needs and resources, and at the same time succeeds in making virtually everyone unhappy. Wealthier districts are bothered by the one-way flow of funds from their communities to the state (called taxes) with minimal aid returning to their schools (in allocations).

Poorer districts, meanwhile, complain that in comparison to wealthier neighbors, much less is spent on them per pupil, even though their children need extra help to compete in the modern world. In reality, since the issues surrounding school funding are such political "hot potatoes," absent a court mandate, little can be expected to change.

In many states, collective bargaining has allowed educators to be paid significantly higher salaries and benefit than they had received several decades ago. However, since the evaluation systems of teachers and administrators are inadequate or nonexistent, more money (salaries and benefits) does not always translate into better educators and improved teaching and learning experiences and activities. And despite protests from some teachers unions, the collective bargaining agreements have frequently not been in the best interests of children.

The fact remains, however, that money well spent, can make a very big difference in the lives of children. Of course, the key is making the dollars "work in direct services" and "teaching-learning"—e.g., driving funds to the classroom for direct instruction and extra help. Going forward, districts need to review their school and classroom expenditure practices and conduct internal audits to see if, where, and how they spend money truly helps children.

In this chapter, we provided numerous "out of the box" concepts of how the funding problems of schools can be reevaluated for the betterment of children. However, we have only scratched the surface. Districts can end their own screwed-up condition by seeking more and better local "out of the box" answers to funding issues. School officials have to consider two issues. First, we need to make sure the money we spend is making a difference in children's lives. Second, we require new ways—so we stop rationalizing that let's continue to do things the way "we have always done it before," We should stop rationalizing for the continuation of funding a practice that has failed to make a difference. In this regard, six suggestions are useful for better funding and more focused, productive spending on our education:

1. We should fund students, based on their needs, a "weighting" system to see that all kids receive what they require to grow and improve.
2. At the school and system levels, we should drive dollars to the classroom, funding from the "bottom" up, not the other way around.
3. Pay teachers for their work and talents, breaking the rigid pay "schedules" of salary levels that are mostly based on graduate degrees earned and years of experience.

4. Create and pay for better higher HI-TECH classrooms, con-
   necting students to the world and to knowledge, rather than
   using out-of-date textbooks and methods that isolate the
   classroom from the changing world around us.
5. Perhaps, too, make dollars follow the kids, a kind of universal
   "voucher," so that students and their families have more options to match the school and educational settings to the
   needs and talents of their children.
6. And our schools need to use weighted student formula (WSF)
   to relate the costs to the real needs and strengths of all children with disabilities, or those too with special needs or talents—and paying for them rationally.

Hence, we must get creative with our education funding, as schools
are a major financial cost to society that pays priceless benefits to
everyone. When it comes to the funding of schools, we can do
better! And children expect us to do so!

Chapter Seven

Ending the Screwed-Up Continuum by Recognizing That the Unachievable Is Achievable

Once upon a time, to even consider the idea that a man could walk on the moon was ridiculous. Only a few years ago, the Internet and the concept that we would all be connected by personal computers belonged in the world of science fiction. If we go back far enough into the early twentieth century, diseases such as small pox and polio terrified our world. The same is true in education. Pockets of small miracles are achievable once dedicated people say that enough is enough. Shear stated,

> When I told the superintendent and the high school cabinet that a 100% graduation rate was achievable, they just politely smiled. I think they were thinking that here he goes again. I said it in the 2002–2003 school year and had little to no support including a lack of funding. I reallocated monies by bringing at-risk kids back from out of district placements and created a program to take care of potential drop-outs. By the 2005–2006 school year we had reached a 99% graduation rate. In 2007–2008 we were among the very few high schools in Ameri-

ca to have a 100% graduation rate. And not fudged numbers, every student who entered our 9th grade graduated on time four years later.

Today, we live in a world in which overcoming the impossible has become commonplace. Given the backdrop of our remarkable journey, the twenty-first century is ripe for the introduction of new and spectacular improvements in education. In a world surrounded by these innovations, we must consider why we have allowed the problems of schooling to remain in the realm of the unsolvable, year after year, and decade after decade.

The authors believe that the perpetual state of "screwed-up" exists because society has never been clear about or dedicated to fixing its public schools. In reality, American society wants it both ways. Educators, parents, students, politicians, the media, and virtually every element of our society want, in fact, demand the fixing of our public schools.

However, they desire a fix to the system and a process that does not really change things very much. All groups seem to want to change, but not too much—make improvements, but without shaking things up. And in the end, the public demands having different results without approaching schooling in a different way. In effect, we want schools to change and remain the same, both at the same time.

Often when discussing school innovations, many wish to go back to yesteryear in which our schools were the finest in the world. Ignorant of history, today's public is not aware that even in the "good old days," many children were served poorly, if at all, by the public schools. We had "the best public schools in the world" simply because the public schools of other countries were worse. Although accurate statistics on the national graduation rate are difficult to find, we acknowledge 1950 arbitrarily as the first year that more than half of eligible American public school students graduated from secondary schools. This low graduation rate is evidence of a long-term systemic problem.

Today, our children are growing up in a multinational environment in which other countries have caught up and in many cases surpassed us in educating their young. As difficult as it is for some reformers to acknowledge, we will not regain an elite place among the world's public schools by emulating others. America is a different society with a unique subset of youngsters. Our children have been raised with very high self-esteem, a fact that is often pointed out in the bashing of our kids. In fact, the claim has been that the only thing that American children are number one in the world at is *self-esteem*. However, high self-esteem can be used in reshaping our schools and moving to the top of the world in student performance.

Confidence is a good thing, not a bad thing, if utilized correctly in the learning process. After all, we all learned to walk with the confidence that we would get it right after the initial process of falling down repeatedly. We will fix our schools only when we recognize that our students are consumers who have been mislabeled. They do not wish to avoid work. In reality our students love to learn. What they hate is boring, redundant, disrespectful pedagogy and curriculum. They don't want to skip school; they want to be at school. What they want to skip is a dangerous world in which predators are allowed to have free reign over them and a world in which adults love them in word but not deed.

Our students are demanding a new set of educators who have been trained in the very refined craft of leading children to think and create on the highest levels. Instead, we are giving children the educators created in colleges and universities that are clueless about a wide range of schooling and human relationship issues. New teachers quickly learn after arriving at their school of employment that effective professional development is for the most part a big joke. The public schools and the universities that produce teachers are like two baseball players simultaneously yelling at each other, "You take it." The ball that subsequently falls to the ground in between is our children's future.

The suggestions we recommend throughout the book are doable and reality based. If we want to fix our public schools—and everyone seems to be in agreement that they need fixing—we must cure the disease. The disease is that we are seeing the schools through paradigms that are simply wrong. The real truth is if we want to fix schools quickly and effectively, we must change the filters we use to see schools.

The *fastest way* to great schools is through new cultural paradigms. The *only way* to create great public schools is through new cultural paradigms. When adults make the statement "What was good enough for us is good enough for our children," they are indicating that they are ignorant that what was "good enough for us" wasn't good enough for us. The older generation has accepted the lie that succeeding in school must come at a personal price. Each year, tens of thousands of American children disagree.

BLIND TO THE REAL PROBLEM

How blind are Americans to the cause of America's perpetual failed effort to reform its public schools? Obviously, very blind, as we continually institute reforms that miss the point. We are the equivalent of George Washington's doctors who couldn't master the concept that sucking the blood from those they were caring for was probably not the best idea. The politicians have demanded accountability testing. It won't work in making our schools the best in the world; but the politicians are riding the back of a tiger. Once they institute the "fix," they can't change direction and they can't get off!

However, we profit little by blaming misguided politicians—or for that matter misguided educators and parents. As much as we want to find individuals and groups to blame because it exonerates us, the fault does not lie with the board members, students, parents, teachers, superintendents, and principals. The problem is in the way the human brain filters information and blinds itself to the truth. We are unable to see the real problem because it defies our common sense. The problem lies with institutional practices that are toxic and immune to the medicines that have been applied. In the area of school reform, it is as if we have been using penicillin to treat a broken back: ridiculous, hopeless, but true all the same.

New solutions for improving our schools, as presented in this book, are out of the norm of how our society thinks. Can the elusive, decades-old missing solution for reforming America's public schools be as simple as viewing students as consumers and therefore pleasing the consumer? Is the failure really all about an angry customer? The truth is that it is about human beings, who can recognize when they are being mistreated—even at a young age.

For many school reformers, even in the twenty-first century, asking kids what they think about their school experience is an alien or missing concept. The problem is this flawed thinking ignores the fact that millions of Americans do that each day. These American trailblazers are called parents, and many begin their afternoon or early evening discussion at home with the inquiry "How was school today?" These parents listen closely to stories of inept pedagogy, meaningless curriculum, poor relationships, fear of other kids, and verbal abuse at the hands of school officials. Tens of thousands of parents and students go to bed each night unhappy with a system that they are impotent to change. The system is simply bigger than they are!

Even today, using market research indicating "student satisfaction"—as a critical benchmark and lever to reform America public schools—would be considered the height of absurdity by the majority of reformers and school officials. The idea of allowing the young to be involved in decision-making would be deemed ridiculous as many critics would be sure that kids would choose lollipops and soda for lunch, playing instead of learning, and sleeping late instead of arriving to school on time. Furthermore, many adults would be sure that a "Lord of the Flies" type of anarchy would arise in schools that are shaped by the ideas of children (as if many of today's schools are safer).

What do many successful and unsuccessful students have in common? More than we would like to consider? The truth is, in varying degrees, students hate the school experience. They are all affected by the way they were made to feel, and for the dropout, having a lower quality of life was considered more acceptable than staying in school.

Research tells us that dropouts understand what is likely to happen to them, and they still leave. In effect, these students do not "drop out," for the process of dropping out is more accurately termed "fading out." Over a period of years, the student's experience is so undesirable that they fight back by being undesirable, unpleasant, disruptive, and absent. As a result, in many cases, educators do not encourage these young people to return to school. In fact, they discourage their return.

Today, evidently, the only American school reform movement that will work is one in which the foundation approach of schools changes. The notion that students must be forced to comply—that schoolwork is inherently displeasing and that children who learn in different ways are bad—must be seen for the erroneous concept it represents. When children are treated well, attend school in pleasing environments, are loved and safe, and are exposed to exciting pedagogy and meaningful curriculum, school outcomes will soar. This achievement will also appear on the meaningless, foolish standardized tests that American politicians and educational leaders have come to embrace.

A NEW CALL FOR ACCOUNTABILITY

The present educational reform movement is accountability based. However, the methodology used for measuring accountability is flawed. In the future, someone will write a book about incredulous thinking; and instead of citing the bloodletting that killed Washington, they will cite the testing of four and five year olds. Districts are under so much pressure to look good in the world of standardized tests that babies have become fodder for the cause.

The strength of the present accountability system is based on competition, public exposure, and consequences for poor performance. We think these ideas are premised on the traditional "blame game" of looking for a scapegoat, when no person or group is wrong in a situation. We see instead wrong thinking that has permeated an entire society. Again, accountability and expectations are fine when they come from a place of love. Today's accountability system comes from a place of fear and confusion.

If the system demands measurements for success, they should be based on multiple factors, including *process-oriented* indicators. We will not get the results that we desire without making sure that the process of schooling is healthy and based on the practices of consumerism. Is the curriculum of a high quality? Do teachers continue to explore and employ exciting pedagogy designed to steer children toward discovery and higher-order thinking skills? Is the school a warm, safe, and loving place for children? Do children have a voice? Would the children choose to come back to the school next year if they had a choice? Can the system replace educators who have proved repeatedly to be substandard?

Students need to be empowered and enter school each day with a true sense of pleasure. But for these qualities to be introduced, fear of change and new systems has to be dealt with. Educators are wonderful people who need to be gently brought into a new way of operating. Their fears should be recognized and considered as change is instituted. However, fear of change can't be a deal break-er.

Students like all people want positive feedback; but more impor-tantly, they want a chance at a better life and a fair system in which they understand what is expected of them. They want to be treated well. The fear of a system that allows student feedback to be the major part of our dialogue can no longer be the reason that schools simply do not improve.

THE FAILURE OF THE LEGISLATORS

Arguably, the number one priority of members of the various state legislatures is to get reelected. When it comes to legislators getting reelected, teachers associations, superintendent groups, and board associations all lobby, and their members can and do vote. As an outcome of the power of these adult-based groups, practices regard-ing the public schools have been designed around the narrow view-point of adults. Although attempts are also made to protect children through educational law, all too often the protections fall far short of their intended purpose. In practice, the protection systems en-acted for adults in the educational system (such as tenure and labor relations laws) are much more effective.

What recourse does a child have when an adult uses arbitrary grading, verbal abuse, humiliation, unfair competition, and un-sound practices? In theory and law, students are protected. In real-ity, they are not, and when they try to be heard, retribution may be waiting. Fear exists even among well-educated parents that coming to the aid of their child may result in arbitrary and capricious pun-ishment toward their child going forward.

High on Maslow's hierarchy of needs is *safety*. When schools are unsafe, do the students have any real protection? Can they really turn to the administration for help? In some states, legislators have responded to unsafe schools with bureaucratic reporting to identify unsafe schools. Today in New York State, administrators have to fill out forms on violence and other issues within the school. Has this helped schools? Do children feel safer? The reality is that to protect children with more administrative reporting is foolish.

We do not underestimate the difficulty in balancing protections within the schoolhouse for the victim and the accused. But we believe that the legislators really have not made their best effort and are falling short in helping create safer schools. As we've noted, if they faced violence in the halls and bathrooms of the legislature, legislators would better understand the student experience.

Absent from the legislation in most states are laws aiding the reasonable removal of children who evidence dangerous and preda-tory behavior. Also missing from legislation is help for students who are placed in class with other children who constantly disrupt and steal valuable educational time. Legislators should hold hear-ings with children and find out first hand what life in school is like. And when they find the truth, instead of their traditional cop-out—that of blaming school officials—they should realize that the solu-tions are complicated. However, on this issue, the legislatures have the power to improve the lives of children in school. It is time they step up and implement the type of needed changes.

ECONOMIC INEQUITY BY LAW

States have allowed certain schools, in certain neighborhoods, to operate in substandard conditions. The legal position has always been that these schools are not guaranteed equal funding under the law.

The federal government has spent a fortune bailing out banks, both in this century and in the savings and loan debacle of the 1980s. The reality of government in the United States is we always seem to have money to do what the politicians want to do when they want to do it. Few Americans were presented with what we could have had if we didn't spend our wealth on fighting in Iraq and Afghanistan. But we most certainly could have had shining, fantastic schools.

Perhaps the next time the government looks to spend a fortune on their latest "must do," we may consider how we could spend our money to make schools better. Perhaps that better spending could help to create schools that are remarkable and worthy of our children. But for the time being, we should remember that the traditional position of our government is that schools are not guaranteed equal funding under the law.

SCHOOLS OF EDUCATION AND PROFESSIONAL DEVELOPMENT

Schools of education produce candidates who are neither ready to teach nor aware of the concepts we have articulated in this book. Schools of education must center their curriculum on advanced pedagogy, comprehensive knowledge of the subjects to be taught, intricate knowledge of human behavior, recognition that a teacher's job is to provide service, and relationship training. Lots and lots of relationship training.

Additionally, many schools of education hire professors based on prestigious résumés. School superintendents who retire often get positions in these graduate schools and then bring in other retired superintendents. These individuals may be very knowledgeable about the holistic issues of education but are they really experts on pedagogy? Do they really understand relationships? Are they really at the stage of their life in which they are eager to make a difference? The hiring of professors in schools of education needs to be reconsidered based on a new philosophy of professional development. The question is, "Do they get it?" And do they know what to do about it?

Once hired into the public schools, teachers can easily tell us that professional development is nonexistent or substandard and often based on the latest fad. But since professional development is offered so infrequently, the fact that the program misses the mark is the least of the problem.

Professional development must improve, and teachers associations should cooperate with the increased time allocated outside their standard contracts dedicated to professional development. The continued education of teachers is crucial to the improvement of schools. All too often, educators consider themselves a "finished product" upon receiving tenure. All too often the finished product is not finished and, on occasion, far from it.

Professional development must be centered on the core principles of improved education. These include relationship training, improved pedagogical practices, curriculum expertise, and a curriculum based on higher-order thinking skills. Professional development has to be great or it is irrelevant; teachers have little patience for substandard pedagogy and curriculum—even if on occasions they employ it themselves, in their own classrooms. Teachers associations must agree to extensive professional development training during non-instructional time.

UNFORESEEN CONSEQUENCES

We virtually never consider the consequences of educating our children in the type of school systems we employ. Today, competition is at the core of our foundation belief about what makes a successful school. However, we have always used a system based on "winners and losers," and the individual's success often comes at the expense of others.

Our educational system spends very little time on relationship training. Many teachers are natural models of good behavior; however, some are not. The system rarely deals effectively with teachers who evidence poor behavior and have marginal relationships with their students. As far as how children treat each other, the dialogue regarding this interaction is often missing from the schoolhouse. Even when it is employed, the discussion usually is on a hit-or-miss basis, lacking consistency.

As a society, we are perplexed as we have a rampant bullying problem within our schools. A reported thirty-thousand kids miss school each month in the United States as a result of bullying. We have a society that produces too many bankers, CEOs, and politicians who legally manipulate the systems and care little about others. We need to consider what part of the negative behavior of adults stems from their education within the American public schools and from topics and concepts of behavior that were explored in insufficient depth.

Our children learn what we model. We model bullying when a teacher can arbitrarily act, year after year, decade after decade, in ways that are reprehensible. And although it is politically correct to say that the overwhelming number of teachers do not behave in this manner—and while that is true—few students will also report at the end of their public education that they have not been bullied by a least one teacher during their school career.

We teach our children to "go along to get along." We do not challenge systems that hurt our children; and in doing so, we teach another generation that justice, even in the great United States, is a moving target. We advocate that everyone speak on behalf of making children's lives better. But what is true in rhetoric is simply not true in reality or in action.

If we desire a moral society, one that evidences personal responsibility, we must model it in our public schools. We should begin this effort by creating a social justice system in schools that allows children to be treated with love and respect. The unintended consequence of our failure to fix our public schools is a society in which we are often unhappy with the actions of others. Perhaps the next generation of public schools will *not* produce people with the morality of Bernie Madoff. We will have a much better chance if we make the concept of exploring social conscience a reality in our public schools.

SUMMARY

We live in a world where the impossible has become the commonplace. Therefore, the changes we recommend are doable and reality based. Without question, our schools must be centered on love and not fear. We must consider that our public schools must operate on a constant basis of "reasonableness." Whenever we have disagreement—or confusion upon the direction we should take—we must employ the concept of what reasonable people would decide and do in this situation.

Our students must be seen clearly and accurately. For the most part, children are not lazy and uninterested students who do not want to work and would love to skip school. They are, too often, dissatisfied with the product that we offer them. They do not want to go to a place that bores them, makes them feel bad, and all too often is unsafe. They want to be educationally challenged on a level appropriate to their ability. They also want to be treated as if they are important!

Perhaps if we used the Golden Rule regarding our children, we would be fine. We would not do onto ourselves what we have done onto them. We would not want to sit day after day in conditions that are among the worst in our society. We would not want to work in offices in which we could be mugged by going into the hall or the bathroom. We would not like to be lectured at for hours each day. We would not want to be prohibited from problem-solving with our colleagues. We would not prefer to be told in a variety of ways that to be successful, we are best served by keeping our mouths shut and going along with bad and harmful practices.

Most importantly, we need to recognize that schools are not fixed by holding on to the practices that were broken in the first place. Certain groups and individuals will be truly angered by the suggestion of change. But so were the British on a particular day in Boston in the 1770s. When change comes, some groups will fight every step of the way to prevent it. But we need to embark on change before we all wind up in the water surrounded by "tossed tea."

Chapter Eight

Ten Changes to End the Screwed-Up Continuum

Schools run on unquestioned foundations that are considered so unimpeachable that to violate them is unthinkable. But let's consider that some of these foundations are cracked, and changes were implemented as a result. Too many books on education offer theoretical recommendations that lack practical application. We offer ten game-changing actions that can be pursued immediately to end the screwed-up continuum.

Change Suggestion 1. Lotteries for Class Choice. In today's educational system, children are assigned to teachers' classes by administration. We recommend that schools operate on the principle of a market economy. In other words, replace the administration-directed method of class placement with choice. And where too many students want a particular teacher or program, then a lottery system will allow parents and students to pick teachers based on winning the lottery, as many urban charter schools now do.

Through the process, if a teacher is at the bottom of the selection process over a number of years, that teacher is retrained or replaced. As such, state tenure laws should be revised to fit within the concept of consumerism combined with professional review. (And lottery spots would have to be balanced based on special education needs.)

Change Suggestion 2. Lotteries for School Selection. The same lottery system can be used for selecting schools. Districts should group schools into categories and let parents select through a lottery. Schools that finish last (at the bottom of everyone's choice list over a number of years) could have the principal fired, a large percentage of the staff replaced, and a redesign to improve the classes and programs for children.

Change Suggestion 3. Bonus Pay Votes. Let parents and students vote on bonuses for educators who make a difference, based on the concept of teachers going the extra mile for children. The areas of consideration can include the following: extra help, creation of materials and learning aids, communication with parents, motivating a student's desire to attend school, and helping to foster a loving environment.

Change Suggestion 4. Parent Report Cards. With more rights come more responsibility and more accountability. Educators will constantly point to inappropriate parents and their effects on the system. Rarely do parents consider how much their rights are being ignored, violated, and curtailed as a result of other inappropriate parents. A suggested remedy is a parent report issued by educators to a review panel to review if the parental behavior was reasonable.

Judgment would be based on appropriateness of relationships, reactions to educators' attempt to communicate, responses to their child's discipline situation, and home support of the child's educational needs. Most importantly, the parents must evidence respectful treatment and demeanor even when dealing with educators with whom the family disagrees.

Presently, the school system, community, and other parents are paying a very high price for the few inappropriate parents. Controlling them can make a major difference in the running of schools. A parent with a repeated bad rating can be referred to government agencies and be mandated to counseling. Financial penalties for bad parenting would be a novel idea for legislators to consider. Obviously, safeguards will be needed to protect parents from vengeful educators. However, holding parents accountable—and giving them help with the education of their children in a democracy—is long overdue.

Change Suggestion 5. Exit Report Cards. Parents in consultation with their children should issue a final report card to the school upon their child's graduation, based on key variables. The variables should be dominated by the affective domain and treatment. A combination grade for the school can be compiled by the Parent Advocacy Group and posted publicly. Again, individual educators will need to be protected from cheap shots and unfair attacks. However if done right, this approach could be a valuable component in improving the treatment that students and parents receive at their schools.

Change Suggestion 6. Transparent Mastery Grading of Students. Parents and children should be provided with a clear matrix of how their child's grade will be compiled. Additionally, parents and students should proactively be provided with a grading rubric for every writing, reading, and math assignment and project. Most importantly, schools need to be converted to a system in which each student must master the work before proceeding. A student who receives a failing grade indicating a lack of mastery needs the opportunity to "learn the work" and have "some relief" from the failing grade.

Change Suggestion 7. Superintendent/Board of Education Accountability. Board of education members and superintendents should be held accountable for the same concepts of consumer satisfaction as teachers and principals. The free pass granted to school leaders by state legislators and communities should end immediately.

The ability to make final decisions should be accompanied by ultimate responsibility. The board of education must create a school system based on love and not fear. And when the district leadership fails repeatedly to set up appropriate schools, government must step in and declare a "district in distress." A "district in distress" would have mandated outcomes required of its leaders or they would face removal from their position.

Change Suggestion 8. Consumer Influence on Curriculum and Courses in Schools. Parents and students should have the right to influence curriculum and elective courses, based on their desire for learning and the needs of the students. Presently, curriculum and electives are influenced by cultural norms and educators' talents or interests.

Too often parents and students are shackled with a mandated course that might have made sense at one time but has long passed its usefulness. Educators fail to revisit curriculum due to multiple factors. Changing curriculum could affect staffing needs and influence educators' jobs. Additionally, busy educators will often place changing the curriculum on the bottom of their "to do list." One PTA president on Long Island stated:

> The school district decided to have every student take a mandated science research course as freshman. This effectively curtailed all freshmen who were interested in both art and music to take one and not the other. For many children this was a terrible loss. What is worse is the science teachers really didn't want to teach the course and it was really not very good. Four years after parents brought this problem to the attention of the school and district administration, nothing has changed.

Change Suggestion 9. Integration of Parental Feedback in College Counseling. Parent-initiated changes in the college counseling process are long overdue. In virtually every school district, parents can narrate a list of things they wish they had known but only learned after their child had gone through the college application process.

School districts are often not very responsive to parent needs in this area. The process has been dominated by educators defensively saying that they are doing a good job, as parents point to important gaps in parental knowledge about a crucial issue regarding the college process.

Change Suggestion 10. A Revamp of Professional Development and College Preparation. Educators fall short in three critical areas: social-emotional understanding, curriculum expertise, and pedagogy. Students report that classes are often boring and unimaginative and sometimes evidence the teachers' lack of concern for students as people. We call for an immediate change to revamp these three important areas in teacher development and to improve assessment, review, and reporting to parents. Additionally, educator assessment as a consumer-based system may use these three variables as a framework for evaluation.

Thus, we seek to make schools more human, personal, and loving places where our children can grow and expand their worldview, and where teachers are their "parents at large," helping them to succeed. A school in Westminster, Maryland, was and is remembered this way.

Many students who attended Robert Moton High School remember it as a loving place. The conditions were awful—winters were cold. Students wore coats in class, although there was a furnace. The furnace was going full blast, but the room was still cold. Sidney Sheppard remembers reading from used textbooks and sitting at battered desks, handed down after white students had finished using them.

"We didn't have the same facilities as the other students, that was obvious," Richard Dixon said. "But the students had each other and family. They worked together to create a loving caring educational atmosphere."

SUMMARY

From the onset of the nineteenth century, American public schools have seen many successes. Accurately stated, the creation of the public schools has made America's desire for an egalitarian society possible. However, many students never found success as a result of their schools. Educational institutions failed to help them achieve their dreams, as they had to find better lives through other venues—or not at all.

In fixing problems, we have to acknowledge that the past does not equal the future. Just because things are a certain way, or have been the practice over many generations, does not validate their effectiveness now or in the future.

Poor practices have been evident in the American public schools since their inception. Creating a "false positive" within a highly flawed system happened because educators of excellence—and a segment of the population—were hungry for success. They often made even the worst practices look good. Hence, we have been under an illusion about the so-called good old days in the public schools that never existed.

Thomas Friedman (2008) describes today's world as hot, flat, and crowded. And the public schools that have sustained us for a century and a half are no longer good enough in this changing world. Global competition is fierce, so sustaining and improving the American lifestyle requires a new approach, especially from its public schools.

Meeting the needs of the consumer—thus improving professional development and leading with love instead of fear—is powerful medicine for an ailing system. In *The Black Swan*, Nassim Nicholas Taleb (2010) details how the future is not predictable based on past events. As Americans, we have been writing an unpredictable but successful script for over two centuries.

We can do it again. This is a changing world, and we now require new approaches to the public schooling of our children. Out-of-the-box thinking by Americans landed men on the moon, created the personal computer, and established the Internet. Different thinking will and can also save our schools. The authors of *Screwed-Up School Reform* are betting on the American people.

We are confident that board members, superintendents, teachers, parents, students, union officials, and even elected leaders will thus consider the recommendations in *Screwed-Up School Reform* and that they will make the right choices. We believe great school days are ahead. We believe that the American promise of a better life as a result of the public schools is a promise that can be met.

References

A Nation at Risk: The Imperative for Educational Reform. (1983). Washington, DC: National Commission on Excellence in Education.

Berne, R., & Stiefel, L. (1999). Concepts of school finance equity: 1970 to the present. In *Equity and adequacy in education finance: Issues and perspectives.* H. F. Ladd, R. Calk, & J. S. Hansen, eds. Washington, DC: National Academy Press, pp. 7–33.

Bill and Melinda Gates Foundation. (2006). *The Silent Epidemic: Perspectives of High School Dropouts.* John Bridgeland et al. New York: Civic Enterprises.

Brandt, R. (1995). Punished by rewards? A conversation with Alfie Kohn. *Educational Leadership, 53*(1), 13–16.

Brooks, J. G., & Brooks, M. G. (1993). *The case for constructivist classrooms.* Alexandria, VA: Association for Supervision and Curriculum Development.

Brown v. Board of Education of Topeka, 347 U.S. 483, 1954.

Carlson, R. O. (1962). *Executive succession and organizational change: Place bound and career bound superintendents of schools.* Chicago: Midwest Administrative Center, University of Chicago.

Chubb, J. E., and Moe, T. M. (1990). *Politics, markets, and America's schools.* Washington, DC: Brookings Institution.

Cooper, Bruce S. (2005). From courtroom to classroom: Operationalizing "adequacy" in funding teaching and learning. In *Yearbook of the American Education Finance Association,* 2005.

Cooper, B. S., & Mulvey, J. D. (2012). *Interconnections of children's health, education, and welfare.* New York: Palgrave Macmillan Press.

Dodd, A. W. (1995). Engaging students: What I learned along the way. *Educational Leadership, 53*(1), 65–67.

Elam, Stanley M., ed. (1978). *A decade of Gallup polls of attitudes toward education: 1969–1978.* Bloomington, IN: Phi Delta Kappa.

Etzioni, A. (Ed.) (1969). *The semi-professions and their organizations.* New York: The Free Press.

Friedman, T. (2008). *Hot, flat and crowded: Why we need a green revolution.* New York: Picador.

Gabor, A. (1990). *The man who discovered quality—W. E. Deming.* New York: Random House.

Gibson, J. L., Ivancevich, J. M., & Donnelly, J. H. (1979). *Organizations.* New York: Harper & Row.

Glasser, W. (1986). *Control theory in the classroom.* New York: Harper & Row.

————. (1990). The quality school. *Phi Delta Kappan, 71*(6), 425–35.

Goble, H. (1970). *The third force—The psychology of Abraham Maslow.* New York: Grossman.

Goodlad, J. (1984). *A place called school.* New York: McGraw-Hill.

Hill, P. T., Roza, M., & Harvey, J. (2008). *Facing the future: Financing productive schools.* Bothell, WA: Center on Reinventing Public Education, University of Washington.

Jensen E. (2005). *Teaching with the brain in mind.* Alexandria, VA: Association for Supervision and Curriculum Development.

Kohn, A. (1993). *Punish by reward: The trouble with gold stars, incentive plans, A's, praise, and other bribes.* Boston: Houghton-Mifflin.

Likert, R. (1967). *The human organization: Its management and value.* New York: McGraw-Hill.

Lortie, D. (1975). *Schoolteacher: A sociological study.* Chicago: University of Chicago Press.

Lott, J. G. (1995). When kids dare to question their education. *Educational Leadership, 52*(7), 15–19.

Marzano, R. J. (2003). *What works in schools: Translating research into action.* Alexandria, VA: ASCD.

McGregor Burns, J. (1978). *Leadership.* New York: Harper & Row.

National Commission on Excellence in Education. (1983). *A nation at risk: The imperative for education reform.* Washington, DC: Author.

National Education Goals Panel. (1993). *Summary guide to the national education goals report: Building the best.* Washington, DC: Author.

Nieto, S. (1994). Lessons from students on creating a chance to dream. *Harvard Educational Review, 64*(4), 392–426.

Noblit, G. W., Rogers, D. L., & McCadden, B. M. (1995). *In the meantime: The possibilities of caring.* Phi Delta Kappan, 76, 680-85.

Noddings, N. (1992). *Challenge to Care in Schools: An Alternative Approach to Education.* New York: Teachers College Press.

Pierce, B. N., & Stein, P. (1995). Why the monkey passage bond: Tests, genre, teaching. *Harvard Educational Review,* 65(1), 50-65.

Ratey, J. (2008). *Spark.* New York: Little, Brown and Company.

Serrano v. Priest, 5 Cal. 3d 584 (1971).

Schott Foundation for Public Education. (2010). *Yes We Can: The Schott 50 State Report on Public Education and Black Males*. Cambridge, MA: the author.

Shanker, A. (1990). The end of the traditional model of schools—And a proposal for using incentives to restructure our public schools. *Phi Delta Kappan, 71*(5), 344–57.

Shear, R. (1996). Measuring student involvement and participation in decision making in public schools (doctoral dissertation, Fordham University, 1996).

Silberman, C. (1970). *Crisis in the classroom: The remaking of American education*. New York: Random House.

Sizer, T. R. (1993). *Horace's school: Redesigning the American high school*. Boston: Houghton Mifflin.

Soo Hoo, S. (1993). Students as partners in research and restructuring schools. *Educational Forum, 57*(3), 386–93.

Stein, A. (1971). Strategies for failure. *Harvard Educational Review, 41*(2), 133–79.

Sylvan Learning Institutes and the National Association of Secondary School Principals. (1992). *Voices from the classroom*. Reston, VA: Author.

Taleb, N. (2010). *The black swan*. New York: Random House.

Tavris C., & Aronson, E. (2007). *Mistakes were made*. Orlando, FL: Harcourt.

Taylor, A. (1993). How schools are redesigning their space. *Educational Leadership, 51*(1), 36-41.

Weeres, J., & Poplin, M. (1992). *Voices from the inside—A report on schooling from inside the classroom*. Claremont, CA: Institute for Education in Transformation at the Claremont Graduate School.

About the Authors

Richard G. Shear, EdD, is an award-winning educator and a national consultant on school reform. He has advised school districts, universities, and educational organizations on numerous issues, such as understanding the teenage brain, preventing bullying in schools, what great teachers do differently, improving school discipline and safety, and saving at-risk students. Over the last decade, his On-Time Graduation Program stands out as one of the most successful anti-dropout programs in the country.

Bruce S. Cooper, PhD, is professor of school leadership at the Fordham University Graduate School of Education. A graduate of the University of Chicago, he has authored thirty books and numerous articles, has served as president of the Politics of Education Association, and has been an active member of the American Educational Research Association (AERA).